SETTING THE STAGE

Early Plays of St. John Paul II

Translated by Bolesław Taborski

Commentary by Kenneth L. Schmitz

CATHOLICPSYCH
PRESS

Cover design by Ann Champagne *@ann.champagne.art.and.design*

Image credit: Young Karol Wojtyla (cover): CNS photo/Catholic Press Photo; "Ecce Homo" (pg. 56): Courtesy of Wikimedia Commons.

E-book: ISBN-13 979-8-9880192-0-6
Hardcover: ISBN-13 979-8-9880192-1-3
Softcover: ISBN-13 979-8-9880192-2-0

CatholicPsych Press
Stamford, Connecticut
www.catholicpsych.com

CONTENTS

PUBLISHER'S PREFACE

A preface can not do justice to what words are capable of in their fullest form. The Word breathed being into life, and the words of John Paul II molded meaning from mystical insight. His form was not breath, but Rhapsodic Theater, forged in the crucible of life and death during Communist rule.

I've the blessing of being one of the "JP2 Generation," and my own reversion to the faith was during the Jubilee year St. John Paul II called for in 2000. His access to the truth of human love and his ability to express it made sense of my own longing as I read *Love and Responsibility*, then the Theology of the Body audiences—no different than most other Catholics my age who care to identify as such. What is not so well known is the earlier work of JP2, which I had the added blessing of being introduced to by the late Dr. Kenneth Schmitz. The Catholic University of America Press has graciously allowed us to reprint his chapter that gives context for these plays within the wider framework of St. John Paul II's entire Personalistic philosophy. It was through the interpretation of Dr. Schmitz that I came to understand how tremendously important these plays are and have, in that light, the greatest excitement at being able to present two of these great works for you here. We are also grateful to the estate of Bolesław Taborksi, the original translator approved by St. John Paul II himself for the English version, for permission to reprint them here.

In our CatholicPsych Certification we start with these plays, as anyone attempting to learn how to accompany others must understand what we're made for and how we're made. Anyone striving to understand the origins of St. John Paul II's ideas about the human person at all should also read these two plays. They present the beauty of the creation of God, "made in His image," made to become more through human action as we journey towards that destiny we're all created for.

Let there be no confusion—the words you hold in your hand are more than words. They are the fruit of deep mystical prayer. They are the movement of the Holy Spirit in the man who would become pope. These words will move you also if you read them with a prayerful heart. If you are of the JP2 generation, you will once again remember the smile and voice of our formative Vicar of Christ. If you are not, meet him here in his most raw, youthful, and yet piercing wisdom.

Dr. Greg Bottaro
March 25, 2023

OUR GOD'S BROTHER

by Fr. Karol Wojtyła (Pope John Paul II), 1945–1950

translated by Bolesław Taborski

INTRODUCTION

This will be an attempt to penetrate the man. The character is strictly historical. Nonetheless, between the man and the attempt to penetrate him there runs a line inaccessible to history. For it is characteristic of man in general that it is not possible fully to fathom him historically. Indeed, an extra-historical element in man lies at the very sources of his humanity. And any attempt to penetrate the man is connected with reaching to these sources.

This "reaching," inasmuch as it is bound, to some extent, to steer free of historical details, will leave something to be desired. For our attention must always be drawn to fact, the fact of humanity—and concrete humanity at that; we assume that this fact is not exclusively historical any more.

Such is the basis of our study. The fact of humanity is carefully scrutinized. But is our study, perhaps, wrong all the same? That is possible. Having set off from the assumptions outlined above, we expect to arrive at no more than a form of probability. Probability, however, is always an expression of the truth one has searched for; what matters is how much real truth it contains. And that depends on the intensity and integrity of the search.

This is where we find ourselves in direct proximity to our hero. In the awareness of each of us his character stands against a rich background, saturated with multifarious reality. He is connected to us by the circle of that reality and through it becomes close and indispensable to us. This too makes us reach to the concrete resources of his humanity, to find in them that peculiar flash of light against the dark background of the reality that connects him to us.

To what degree shall we be able to reveal that light and at the same time preserve it in the raw material of expression available to us? I think we can succeed to the extent that we are able to participate in the same multifarious reality in which he participated—and in a way similar to his.

Dramatis Personae[1]

MAX, a painter

STANISLAW, a painter and art critic

MADAM HELENA, an actress

HER HUSBAND

LUCIAN, a friend of Adam's

GEORGE, a friend of Adam's

MESSENGER from the city council

THEOLOGIAN, Father Casimir, a Jesuit priest

OLD LADY, his mother

STRANGER

ADAM CHMIELOWSKI, later BROTHER ALBERT, called BROTHER SUPERIOR

PEOPLE in the POORHOUSE

VOICE of the OTHER

BEGGAR at the lamppost

PRIEST who hears Adam's confession

MARYNIA, Adam's sister

JOSEPH, Adam's uncle

BROTHER ANTHONY

BROTHER SEBASTIAN

BROTHER STEFAN, the cook

BROTHER JANITOR

YOUNG MAN, called HUBERT

OLD MAN, a brother in the shelter for the poor

BROTHER COLLECTOR

BROTHERS in the shelter for the poor

1. List prepared by the editor

I. The Studio of Destinies

[The location and dimensions of this place will become clear in the course of the action. The people who will pass through it are, after all, a group remembered from history. But what matters most here is their destinies—the development of their destinies.

The two men who are now talking remain in the nearer and better-lit part of the studio.]

MAX

The newspapers are writing about your exhibition already.

STANISLAW

Yes, I saw them this morning.

MAX

In my opinion they will cut you to pieces.

STANISLAW

That's what I expect . . .

MAX

You antagonize everyone. That's not the way.

STANISLAW

Have you ever considered, Max, that we can transform little—ridiculously little—apart from ourselves? As artists we merely try to understand, or rather heed—you know what I mean—and reflect in our work an unexpected insight into our self, which, slowly transformed, has suddenly realized its own transformation. Then people come along, take an interest in the work of art, and through that work engage the artist who can so change his skin like a chameleon. They need this kind of engagement. It means they can transcend themselves. And for that matter, it does not cost them much.

MAX

I envy you such a viewpoint. You have quite a high opinion of your public. I must admit I would find it quite difficult to cope with something like that.

STANISLAW

Well then, why . . .

MAX

You want to ask me, I suppose, why I paint at all. Well, certainly not for the public.

STANISLAW

I wouldn't dare pose the question like that. And yet, in spite of everything, a relation remains, a reference, a social mission.

MAX

Then dissolve it on the palette, give it a coat of oil, and seal it with plaster! And now maybe you will add a word about responsibility . . .

STANISLAW

Ah yes, I think so.

MAX

Excuse me—how big a responsibility?

STANISLAW

How big? . . . I won't reply to that, Max. I think the question is too personal. Besides, we know each other too well, and I have no desire to posture before you.

MAX

Well then—how wide?

STANISLAW

To that I will reply. Yes. I am convinced about the mission of art.

MAX

What mission? From the eyes to the brush. In saying that I do not wish to compare art with craft. Oh no, not at all. But one mustn't exaggerate. I value art to the extent that it stimulates me, gives me the impetus to which my true self inclines. And thanks to that, it tests how much can still be drawn from myself. After all, how a man's self works, how it grows and declines, is extremely interesting. But that is all. All. What more do you want? That is sufficient meaning. Around me, in others . . .?

STANISLAW

You're diminishing, diminishing it, Max. For in reality something slowly grows around you, gathers momentum, widens. Of course, though you have a part in it, you are not the only originator of this mystery. That much is clear.

MAX

You are wrong, Stach. Your mistake begins very close to your art. Do you think it is surrounded by something more than a circle of false and contradictory associations?

STANISLAW

We're not talking about coteries, of course.

MAX

Oh no, we're not talking about coteries—or about snobs. We are talking about the most honest spectator or listener there is . . . Do you think that the citizen of Shoemakers' Street or Vistula Street, who brews beer, or cobbles shoes, or even pores over thirteenth-century manuscripts—that he will be able to re-create in himself the whole truth of your associations, your vision, your agonizing?

STANISLAW

It's independent of that.

MAX

What do you mean—independent of that? If it's independent, then don't blab about influence, effect, mission, and, above all, about responsibility. If it's independent, then all these things don't count.

STANISLAW

Oh, you quibble.

MAX

To a degree—rightly so. For that matter it's all I need to prove my argument. *[*STANISLAW *wants to interrupt]* Wait. Let me finish. You see, there is a multitude, simply a multitude of atoms, revolving each in its own area and range. I too revolve in my area and range. That's all. Whom does it concern? I think I would go to waste if in the course of that spinning movement of my self, I were to take note of actions, influences, and responsibility all the time.

STANISLAW

And yet you too have exhibitions.

MAX

It's a custom. Besides, some part of our self yearns for applause.

STANISLAW

Which you scorn at the same time?

MAX

Oh yes. In every one of us there resides both a man exchangeable like money and, in his innermost depths, a non-exchangeable man known only to himself.

STANISLAW

And what will you do with the exchangeable one? After all, you're not making him a fortune?

MAX

Of course not. But I don't intend to fight him either. It's enough for me simply to be aware of the other, the non-exchangeable one, and to know that within me there is a dividing line between the two. Otherwise life would become commonplace and stupid.

STANISLAW

But if you did fight the exchangeable one?

MAX

That would be unbearable. It is enough to be aware of him. And through awareness to be separate from him.

STANISLAW

Interesting. It will not surprise you, Max, if I tell you that this conversation makes you a mystery to me.

MAX

Not at all.

[Through the half-open door at the back of the studio MADAM HELENA *and her* HUSBAND *have entered somewhat earlier. They have been moving very quietly, unnoticed, from painting to painting, occasionally pausing by the easel and whispering to each other. Obviously, they are not strangers in this studio.* MAX *and* STANISLAW *are talking at the other end of the studio, close to the audience, and they still have not noticed the visitors. The studio is fairly deep and, at this time of day, rather dark]*

MADAM HELENA

[For some time now has been following the conversation, still unobserved. Suddenly]

I think you're wrong, Max. Apologies and—good afternoon, gentlemen.

[Both surprised]

MAX

Good afternoon. You're both here? *[They stand apart]* Allow me to introduce our friend. He arrived last night from Munich for his exhibition. *[They exchange nods]*

MADAM HELENA'S HUSBAND

Ah, it's your exhibition. I read about it in this morning's papers.

*[*STANISLAW *bows his head again]*

MAX *[Mastering an unclear situation]*

As you can see, or rather hear, Stach has brought much idealism in his heart, but I, an old hand and renegade, am bent on rooting it out. But maybe you didn't hear our conversation? . . .

MADAM HELENA

Yes, I heard. And I think you're wrong, Max.

MAX

In that case, madam, I must yield. I am dealing with a privileged person, with whom I cannot disagree. I accept my defeat at once.

MADAM HELENA

No, not for that reason. It just isn't as you say.

MAX

You will forgive me, but the matter is extremely difficult to grasp.

MADAM HELENA

But what you profess, what you are proclaiming, means retreating from art. Truly.

MAX

And even if this were so, do I not have the right to such an experience?

MADAM HELENA

Of course. But one can hardly prove something convincingly if one hasn't done the experiment yet.

MAX

You are entitled to your opinion.

MADAM HELENA

Oh yes, I am deeply convinced of that. You may not realize this, Max, but we are really concerned here with a secret exchange, a mutual participation.

STANISLAW *[Interrupts]*

Max will want to mention right away what he thinks about the so-called exchange, or rather, about the exchangeable man.

MAX

I will be bold enough to add that we are also concerned with a certain responsibility.

MADAM HELENA

You can't be serious.

MAX

But I am. I'm just following your line of reasoning.

MADAM HELENA

Ah, then you were not joking. Thank you. I marvel at your capacity to enter someone else's train of thought. *[She laughs]* And at the same time you—you deny the participation to which your art admits others; you deny the influence you exert on their lives.

MAX

Yes, at the same time I—I deny that influence and that participation and that exchange, Madam Helena.

MADAM HELENA

And yet you know so well how to join and participate in the way others think and feel. And with such honesty . . .

MAX

A simple technique of mixing with people. And you must know it is the exchangeable man who does it. And he is neither the most profound nor the most interesting. It is the non-exchangeable man who is the most interesting.

STANISLAW *[Interrupting]*

You see, he's lecturing now. Just as I said he would.

[The door opens quickly. Enter LUCIAN *and* GEORGE*]*

LUCIAN

Good day, gentlemen, Madam Helena.

GEORGE

Is Adam at home?

MADAM HELENA

That's what I was going to ask.

MAX

As a matter of fact, Adam is not at home.

LUCIAN

When is he coming back?

MAX

He should have been back an hour ago. I am waiting for him myself. Since I am an idler by profession, however, I've been killing time while I wait in a futile discussion about the exchangeable and the non-exchangeable man.

GEORGE

Excuse me, what man? . . .

MAX

Non-exchangeable . . .

MADAM HELENA'S HUSBAND [*Interrupts*]

Since Adam is not here, though, maybe we'll come back in an hour or so.

MADAM HELENA

That's right. I expect Adam will be back by then, and you, gentlemen, will have had the chance to draw a clear distinction between non-exchangeable man and the subject of elemental changes.

MAX

That is quite possible. And indeed Adam, the very subject, will no doubt soon appear in a state of absolute non-exchangeability, inaccessible to elements. We will then stop him in his tracks and make him wait for you.

MADAM HELENA'S HUSBAND

Thank you.

[The two of them leave]

LUCIAN

But you are joking, of course . . .

MAX

Not at all.

LUCIAN

Well, I do find it difficult to understand Adam.

STANISLAW

Tell me, Max, does Adam have talent?

MAX

I am fully convinced of that.

GEORGE

Hm . . . It's not quite so straightforward. It's something different. The notion of talent does not express what matters in Adam.

STANISLAW

Then what does?

LUCIAN

I would describe it this way: Adam transforms a great many things within himself and then marks the results on canvas. Don't you see, gentlemen? In my opinion, he is not a typical painter. Try to understand the difference. Each of you tries to find on canvas the various possible and successive solutions to your lives. Your lives happen, take place, on canvas. That's why you can't see them differently; you are bound to your canvas, subordinated to your palette. With Adam it is different. For him the need for canvas and paint drags way behind his deepest being. He turns to them almost reluctantly, almost scornfully because, after all, he regards them as a means and requires them as such. But that is all. His attitude toward his craft is far more detached. He is far more independent. Basically, he lives within himself, develops and contracts in himself, not on canvas. No, no. He is not a typical painter.

GEORGE

Interesting . . .

STANISLAW

Then—what is he?

LUCIAN

He is rather a typical seeker. Not one who rummages for petty things, but a vigorous, even boisterous seeker.

GEORGE

Anyhow, we are all agreed that lately he has changed a great deal.

MAX

I'll tell you a story. It happened a week ago. Lubacki came here—you know, that fat merchant, a provincial nouveau riche. He wanted a portrait. Adam began to expound his new theories about mutual responsibility. In a word, he harped on the rich man's moneybags and tried to convince him that all the beggars of Zwierzyniec and Krakowska Street had the right to share his wealth.[2] The man tried first to turn this into

2. Zwierzyniec is a district of Kraków.

a joke, then to make some polite excuses and so forth. But Adam was implacable. Of course, all the two gentlemen did was talk. Nonetheless, they did not part in a spirit of mutual understanding.

STANISLAW

It is hard even to imagine that Chmielowski's mystic palette could produce the full-fledged image of a rich man . . .

GEORGE

Unless it were a rich man of the Gospel. The distance is indeed considerable.

MAX

So you think it is better for him that he hasn't been painted. Ha, ha . . . it's quite funny. But Adam, Adam . . . *[A knock at the door]* Come in!

MESSENGER FROM THE CITY COUNCIL

Is this where Mr. Chmielowski lives?

MAX

You mean Adam?

MESSENGER

Yes, Adam.

MAX

He is not at home. What is it?

MESSENGER

A note from the head of the Department of Social Welfare.

MAX

Very well. I'll give it to Mr. Chmielowski as soon as he returns. Meanwhile I can assure you confidentially that the welfare department has got itself a formidable inquisitor.

MESSENGER

What does that mean—inquisitor?

MAX

It means someone who will be close at its heels.

MESSENGER

I don't think it's easy to be at the heels of the head of the Department of Social Welfare. Maybe only his excellency the mayor could do it.

MAX

You think so? We'll see whether you are right. Good-bye now.

[The MESSENGER *bows stiffly and leaves, closing the door]*

LUCIAN

I can guess the reason for that visit.

GEORGE

Well . . .

LUCIAN

No. Adam must have been seized, taken. Do you understand? He's possessed.

MAX

Oh yes, and how.

LUCIAN

I think I know how it all began. This is a process, you know, and it advances, accelerates. Well, it happened some time last winter, early spring rather. We were coming back from Count Z's. There were several of us: Leon, Stefan, Adam and myself.[3] Somewhere in Krakowska Street, sleet began to fall sharply, the wind rose, and soon a dense, damp fog swirled about us. Someone said we should wait till it had blown over.

---

3. Leon is most probably Leon Wyczółkowski (1852-1936), a foremost painter of his generation. He befriended Adam Chmielowski when he continued at Kraków from 1877 to 1879 studies begun earlier at Munich. He was a professor at the Academy of Fine Arts in Kraków from 1895 to 1911. Stefan could be Stefan Żeromski (1864-1925), the eminent Polish novelist, who at various times came into contact with Adam Chmielowski.

We took shelter at random in the first doorway. Adam, impatient as usual, started shaking the door handle. Suddenly, the door yielded. Instinctively we all drew back. There was a huge space, almost dark, with only a few gleams of light coming from one or two paraffin lamps that hung from the ceiling; but the light dissipated half way down, and the lower part of the room was dark.

I remember clearly what Adam did then. He moved slowly forward, one, two steps . . . He entered that dark space. We were all standing by the door. I heard his footsteps on the floor. There were no floor boards, just a hard mud floor. Gradually our eyes too got used to the darkness. We saw a number of bunks, or rather shakedowns, made of straw thrown onto boards. People crouched on the edges of the bunks. They were sitting, lying down, swaying, with knees high up by their chins, or folded like crabs. They were smoking cigarettes, playing cards, talking in low voices. But somewhere in a corner there was an argument over a place. Both men and women were there.

Our greatest impression in all this was the hollow sound of Adam's footsteps. He walked between the rows of bunks, as if attracted by an unknown force; he walked from one group of people to another. He took off his wide-brimmed hat and carried it in his hand, crumpling it on his chest. One could hardly see the outline of his figure; I only heard his steps thumping in the dark poorhouse, falling as it were from on high. Thus he walked—followed, no doubt, by their glances, some full of hate, others of curiosity—as if he were a lost person seeking shelter for the first time in that hovel.

Then he came back to us. He looked terrible. In the faint light of the lamp his face seemed to be molded of green wax. His eyes were big and terrified. His soaked beard and hair completed the picture.

I remember telling him, "Adam, the rain has stopped; we can go now." He joined us without a word.

No one dared to turn the conversation back to the splendid evening at Count Z's house. Everyone felt the gulf . . .

STANISLAW

And what did Adam do?

LUCIAN

Adam didn't say a thing. We reached the end of Grodzka Street and took leave of one another without a word. That was his style. But now he has taken it into himself. That, too, is his style.

STANISLAW

Taken it into himself?

LUCIAN

Oh yes, he is reshaping it within himself.

STANISLAW

What will result from it? A new phase in his art? . . .

LUCIAN

I don't know. I've told you what I think about Adam's art. I've told you what I think about Adam.

MAX

One thing is certain: since he has ceased to belong to himself, he has also ceased to belong to his art. He paints distractedly, haphazardly. Sometimes after five minutes he throws down his brush and looks aimlessly at the Vistula. He is clearly shattered. I try to find in him what was there in the Munich days, when that boy seemed so carefree to me, without secrets really, without all those inner twists that gather shadows. And you know, I can't . . . I don't know why, but I sense something new, something strange in him, an element inscrutable to me. *[A knock on the door]* Come in.

[Enter THEOLOGIAN *and* OLD LADY*]*

THEOLOGIAN

Excuse me, is Mr. Chmielowski in?

MAX

He should be here any moment. Meanwhile, can I help you?

THEOLOGIAN

Well, then, would you let us have a look at Mr. Chmielowski's paintings? My mother has just come up from the country. I should like to show her an interesting example of modern religious painting.

MAX

Of course, I don't see why not. I know it has always been Adam's custom to make his studio accessible to anyone. But he doesn't like exhibitions.

THEOLOGIAN

Thank you, gentlemen.

[He withdraws up stage with his mother, and the two of them begin to look at the paintings, sometimes whispering remarks. In the foreground the conversation continues]

MAX

I repeat then, a new element, inscrutable, as far as I can see.

GEORGE

Is it really new?

MAX

I repeat, new to me.

GEORGE

It could have been there before, only not so pronounced, and that's why you didn't feel its resistance. You could simply penetrate a man so constituted, filled with the same ideas as yourself; you could easily go through him . . .

MAX

And now?

GEORGE

Now, everything that had previously been concealed in him, everything that had been latent, as it were, in his human nature, has grown, or rather spread, like the shadow of a planet on the moon.

STANISLAW

And to your eye, Max, to your skilled, unerring painter's eye, there has been a sudden eclipse.

MAX

Maybe . . .

GEORGE *[Returns to his argument]*

But you must not imagine an upheaval in the universe. No, no. This must have taken root in him a long time ago. Everything is rooted in a man. All that is needed is a force to release what was previously hidden.

MAX

Where does this force come from?

GEORGE

I don't know. I have long studied similar manifestations. I have looked for them in people . . . I do not know.

[The conversation in this circle ceases for a while. Some of the men are lost in thought; others have left this subject with obvious relief. All look, quite unnecessarily and without paying much attention, at the nearest of the canvases standing in the studio. The THEOLOGIAN *and the* OLD LADY *also study the paintings. They have now come a little nearer, and one can hear some of their remarks to each other]*

OLD LADY

I do not find here that childlike, almost naive, approach to God that the Pre-Raphaelites had, or Perugino, or Fra Lippo . . . It's rather a wearisome way around.

THEOLOGIAN

Well, yes, but you must admit, Mother, that he is separated from them not only by four, five centuries of history but also by a powerful difference in the way he thinks.

OLD LADY

Yes . . . Besides, all this is somehow strangely closed within him. One can easily see that something transcends him, takes him out of himself, but defining it is much harder. Is it only melancholy or, indeed, something supernatural?

THEOLOGIAN

Oh, look at that Christ, for instance . . . Of course, he is cautious here, but don't you think, Mother, that this is in many respects all the more precious? For it reveals to us the immense tension within the artist. And that has its own force.

OLD LADY

Of course, Casimir, my boy. One can see at once you're a Jesuit. But the others didn't have it easy either.

THEOLOGIAN

Oh, they certainly had much easier access. Just think, Mother, how many obstacles someone who searches as he does must overcome today. That's why I say that apart from the centuries of history, one must take into account the powerful difference in mentality.

OLD LADY

And yet . . . there everything was real and clear. Here—how shall I put it—it's not that everything somehow acquires worth from the artist's personal experience, but it shows rather his experience itself than the object.

[During this conversation the men in the group lost in thought utter a few casual remarks]

GEORGE

Well, what are the prospects for your exhibition?

STANISLAW

I suppose they'll cut me to pieces. Max promises me that most decisively.

MAX

Yes.

LUCIAN

You shouldn't take much notice. How many times have I cut Adam to pieces, who is my close friend. Without censure life would be so boring.

STANISLAW

Of course.

[The door opens quickly. It is ADAM. *He is still speaking to someone outside]*

ADAM

It's here. Remember the number of the house and the floor. You can come tonight, all of you. You can sleep here.

MAX *[To those present]*

This sort of thing happens increasingly often. This is less and less an artist's studio, more and more an asylum for beggars.

*[*ADAM *closes the door slowly. He turns to the group of people in the right corner of the room. The* THEOLOGIAN *and the* OLD LADY *have moved so far in the opposite direction that he may not notice them, or see who they are. The* THEOLOGIAN *at first bows his head slightly in* ADAM'S *direction but, unnoticed, returns to view the paintings, leaving* ADAM *to deal exclusively with his friends on the right]*

THEOLOGIAN

Oh, Mr. Chmielowski is back.

OLD LADY

In that case . . . maybe . . .

THEOLOGIAN

Let's wait a moment.

ADAM *[Walks decisively to the right]*
Good afternoon. *[He is somewhat distracted]*

MAX
You don't recognize your new guest.

ADAM
Of course, Stanislaw. I thought you might turn up any day now. *[Somewhat indifferently]* What news from Munich?

STANISLAW
Christian sends you his greetings.

ADAM
He still remembers me . . . Well, yes. *[The conversation flags a little.* ADAM *begins again, more animated]* Has someone been to see me?

MAX
Who?

ADAM
Well, you should know . . . No, not really. None of you know him. A man of about forty? Dressed in black . . .

MAX
No, no one like that has been here. Only Madam Helena and her husband.

ADAM
Oh yes?

MAX
They will be back any minute. And a messenger from the city council brought you a letter. *[*MAX *points to the table.* ADAM *quickly tears open the envelope, reads the letter.* MAX *taps his forehead]* You also have some other guests, who have come to admire your work.

THEOLOGIAN

[Bows his head conspicuously. His mother does the same]

Good day, Mr. Chmielowski. You will forgive us for having invaded your studio in your absence. But my mother wanted so much to see your paintings.

[It is clear that ADAM *finds it hard to tear himself away from the letter, which he considers important. He rises quickly, takes a few steps forward]*

ADAM

You are welcome. I am much obliged to you, madam, for taking an interest in my modest work, which has never succeeded fully or found a total expression. Please, consider these only as trials.

OLD LADY

They are all the more interesting to us.

ADAM

Thank you.

OLD LADY

But I think we have interrupted you. Will you let us complete our viewing?

ADAM

But of course. I feel honored. *[He returns to his former place, reads quickly]* Yes, it's from the welfare department. Forgive me, but this is ridiculous. In that hovel dozens of people waste away. Always new people, for a large number of inhabitants change from day to day. The regulars are just the core. There aren't many of them, but they are absolute masters of the situation. All the others, who arrive there daily, receive suitable training from them and then reenter the world. What happens to them? Where do the disinherited multitude go when they disperse, scatter? Of course, that's something nobody inquires into. The head of welfare writes here that the poorhouse is all the city can afford right now . . .

But I know this multitude will explode . . . After all, once they leave the poorhouse, they don't become any richer or better.

GEORGE

What can you do?

ADAM *[Continues]*

Society doesn't know what it carries within it. Society is like a sick organism. But a sick organism soon spends itself, reaches its limits and fails; society can hide the disease within for a long time. Or rather, it can hide from the disease. Yes, we are hiding; we escape to little islands of luxury, to the so-called social life, to so-called social structures and feel secure. But no. This security is a big lie, an illusion. It blinds our eyes and stops up our ears, but it will shatter in the end.

GEORGE

In a sense, we can wait for that shattering as long as we live. And then—I repeat—what can you do about it?

ADAM *[Talking as if he has not heard him]*

Each of us goes his own way. Each builds his own nest. Meanwhile, for so many people the road has become too narrow. They have nowhere to stand. They have no patch of ground they can call their own, no slice of bread they can earn, no child they can bring into this world without the certainty that it will be in everybody's way. And in the midst of all this we move, arrogantly confident in the strength of a general system that makes us ignore what cries out to be heard and suppress a justified outbreak. No, no. All of us lack something. I don't yet know what. I'm trying hard to find out. But I know that it is so and that there will be an explosion.

[Enter MADAM HELENA *with her* HUSBAND]

MADAM HELENA

Ah, Mr. Chmielowski is back. *[To* MAX *and* LUCIAN*]* Well, gentlemen? Have you come to a definite conclusion on the subject of the non-exchangeable man?

MAX

Not at all. But here is the man himself. He has been trying to scare us with his arguments about mankind's being threatened from below, eaten up at the roots.

ADAM

Please sit down, Madam Helena, sir. *[Turns quickly to* MAX*]* It's not true, Max. Mankind is not being eaten up at the roots. It is rather like a tree being bitten off at the top. Surely you will not maintain that poverty is distributed like a punishment, a just punishment.

MAX

Well, forgive me . . . but after all, I cannot make the life and lot of another man.

ADAM

You mean you will go your own way, build your little nest, taking advantage of the seemingly secure social system. But if that system fails, if you chance to find yourself at the bottom—what then?

MAX

That view of society is wrong. According to you, it is formed by continuous upheavals and changes. And the individual in society is a particle acted on, either pushed down or lifted up. I don't agree with that. The individual makes himself and joins society as an individual. His task, his mission, is first of all individual. He has individual responsibility. Society's fate depends on whether the individual accomplishes his task, fulfills his mission, meets his responsibility, or makes a mess of it. If he succeeds, society will consist of a greater number of worthy individuals and will be rather more worthy itself. If he fails, you will find in it more and more poorhouses and asylums, which are, of course, antisocial phenomena. They are magnets drawing human wrecks and loafers.

ADAM

There is a great deal of truth in what you say. But you are ignoring one thing, Max. In this situation, what are you to do, what am I to do, what is Stanislaw to do, what is Madam Helena to do? You will all forgive me.

MAX

But I have just explained that. Each is to accomplish his task, to create values—create them out of the resources he finds in life. And because he finds these resources mainly in himself, he must shut himself off from the world. Otherwise he will fritter away what he has. And that would be precisely an antisocial attitude.

ADAM

I thought like that for a long time. I thought so even two months ago. But since then I have seen that that is not enough. We cannot permit a whole mass of people to swarm through the poorhouses, leading almost animal lives, gradually deprived of all awareness except of hunger and fear. No, no!

GEORGE

But what can you do about it? Gentlemen, don't you think that with the turn our conversation is taking, we need a theologian?

Father, could you and your mother join our discussion? We are in a predicament. Adam is standing before a tightly closed door. Slammed shut. What is worse, his every attempt to open it meets with extreme resistance. Adam wants to force his way in. He's doing it with characteristic stubbornness. For the time being his stubbornness serves as a substitute for the necessary strength. But the stubbornness can be exhausted. And then I shall fear for Adam. On the other hand, I cannot completely agree with Max . . .

MAX

Exactly. Most people think and act like you; either they do, or they find themselves in poorhouses. And because of that, the upheaval that Adam senses around the corner does not happen, though indeed it should have happened centuries ago.

And so? I suppose we like things as they are—we are comfortable—and that gives us the right to look at the world in this way.

On the other hand, people who think like Adam are few—fortunately. Such people, guided by their impatient judgment, with all their personal nobility, cause upheavals. And upheavals are a rather antisocial phenomenon.

THEOLOGIAN

I have tried to follow the gist of your argument. I admit that thanks to such upheavals mankind has moved forward rather than sideways, stretched like an army in retreat, and yet shrunk.

LUCIAN

Aren't you going too far, though?

THEOLOGIAN

All the more so in that the difference between you is in fact small, and to see it clearly requires careful scrutiny.

ADAM

All this does not change the nature of things a bit. What matters is that he is perfectly sure of himself and utterly convinced that his attitude is the right one. And I . . . for some time now . . . haven't been able to find my way. *[A knock at the door]* Come in. Ah, it's you. I've been asking about you.

*[*STRANGER *enters]*

Please. These are my friends. Father Casimir, Madam . . .

STRANGER *[Bows from a distance]*

Permit me to view your paintings.

ADAM

As you wish. *[Taking up the interrupted conversation]* I cannot find my way . . . it seems to me—more, I am deeply convinced—that all this is just a continuous running away.

STANISLAW

Running away? . . .

ADAM

Yes, running away.

STANISLAW

From whom?

ADAM

In a certain sense, from oneself. But no. *[He thinks aloud]* After all, Max is himself; he lives in the same world as every one of us. And yet Max does not have to run away, has no feeling of being chased . . . And so this does not mean . . . running away from oneself.

MAX

Of course, it must be running away from responsibility. Yes? I wonder, how can I be made responsible for a citizen who has wasted his life and is now at the bottom?

ADAM

You still think, Max, that the pattern of human poverty corresponds to the pattern of punishment . . . No matter. But this is not just running away from responsibility. It is running away from something, or rather someone, in oneself and in all those people.

THEOLOGIAN

Ah, from someone in yourself and in them?

ADAM

Yes. This running away is a wearisome business. All that I have tried to do so far has been a kind of self-protection. That's why this running away is so painful. Something in me keeps opening up, something that until now was closed, something I guarded but did not know about . . .

For some time now this has been becoming clear and . . . it's chasing me. And I keep running away. I'm not defending myself. I don't know how to defend myself. I feel I ought to go onto the attack. But to do that I would have to change completely . . .

THEOLOGIAN

So, it is a gradual elucidation . . . and a pressure.

ADAM *[After a moment's concentration]*

Yes, one could put it that way. Gradual elucidation—and a pressure. But this lucidity is painful. It hurts more and more deeply.

THEOLOGIAN

And what are you defending? . . .

ADAM

How do I know what I am defending? I am defending my right to see the world in my own way. Not as Max sees it but as most people see it. Isn't that so, George? For a few pennies, for a złoty here, a złoty there—the right to lock up quietly in oneself all those upheavals and tensions. The right to separate oneself from them. To stand calmly by the easel. For a złoty here . . . a złoty there . . . to lock up all the world's upheavals in one's eye, in one's artistic vision.

But all this is good for nothing. For a light will open up again, and one has to run away. Again . . . and again. Elucidation and pressure.

OLD LADY *[Whispers to her son]*

I told you, Casimir. This can be seen quite clearly in his pictures.

THEOLOGIAN *[Looks ahead, but speaks rather to* ADAM*]*

It could be a vocation.

ADAM

To what?

THEOLOGIAN

I don't know. You must keep running away.

ADAM

Yes? *[After a while, as if roused from sleep]* No. Forgive me, all of you. How could I get so mawkish about myself? No. I've been abusing your patience.

Well, what were we talking about? . . . Ah yes . . . There is a great deal of truth in what you say, Max. But you see, not everyone can act the way you do.

MAX

I think you ought to paint at any price. Force yourself.

ADAM

To do that I would have to believe in art as you do!

MAX

And you? . . . Maybe you think you will get rid of the urge to paint? Do you really think that this affair with beggars will result in anything but some new canvases? Oh, they will be very interesting, penetrating, will make a great impression and initiate a new period in your art. And that's all.

MADAM HELENA

And then you will see how fruitful all your anguish has been.

LUCIAN

I am afraid you're wrong, madam . . .

ADAM

I think so too . . .

MADAM HELENA

And I am sure I'm right. All this will acquire meaning, gain its full value. Our experience passes into our work. Eventually, we give the experience to others, immerse them, if I may say so, in the stream of beauty . . .

GEORGE

. . . that flows through us . . . Am I to complete the poet's phrase?[4]

---

4. The passage referred to comes from Zygmunt Krasiński's poetic drama *The Un-Divine Comedy (1835):* "Through you flows the stream of beauty, but you are not beauty." The sentence points to the dichotomy between the perfect work of art and the flawed nature of the person who creates it.

MADAM HELENA

The poet was wrong. I testify against him—with my life, my art.

ADAM

Both are extremely valuable. But—forgive me—in this case they are extremely little.

MADAM HELENA

Little . . . in what sense?

ADAM

Yes, little. I mean . . . you see—with them you cannot pay everything off.

MADAM HELENA

I don't understand.

ADAM

How shall I put it? Well . . . Please tell me, what does it cost you to play Ophelia or Lady Macbeth?

MADAM HELENA

What does it cost? . . . In a way, it costs me all my life. Yes . . . but it is a curious price, a strange ransom. Each time I pay it in full; each time I pay it all over again.

ADAM

Yes, it is indeed a strange ransom . . . *[Suddenly]* Well, you see, madam, I cannot buy myself out at that price.

MADAM HELENA

From whom? Yourself?

ADAM

I am not alone.

[A pause. All are silent, as if concentrating on the last word that has been uttered]

THEOLOGIAN

I see. *[To his mother]* Mr. Chmielowski will surely forgive us for having taken so much of his time.

ADAM

It is rather I who have taken your time.

OLD LADY

We must go now. We wish you every success.

ADAM

Thank you. Thank you very much.

[The OLD LADY *and the* THEOLOGIAN *leave}*

LUCIAN

You must admit, Adam, you're becoming famous. More and more people visit your studio.

MAX

If we include peddlers and beggars, this fame will grow *ad infinitum.*

MADAM HELENA

I must tell you, Adam, we sincerely admire your devotion to the poor.

MAX

Again I have to say I oppose it, though I don't find it easy to say so. But one cannot serve two admirations at once. Ever since Adam, as you say, has devoted himself to the poor, admirable though this devotion is, his work has stood still. Has it ceased to be the expression of his vision? . . .

MADAM HELENA

I think not. No one will be able to deprive him of his vision.

ADAM

You are right, Madam Helena. Sometimes one vision is quite enough . . .

[A pause]

MADAM HELENA

Why didn't you finish your last sentence, Max?

MAX

For nothing now will be able to substantiate that vision. And so I repeat, one cannot serve two admirations at once, Madam Helena.

MADAM HELENA

But if both of them grow, they complement each other in some higher entity.

Well, gentlemen? I'll see you at Stanislaw's exhibition.

STANISLAW

You'll be welcome.

*[*MADAM HELENA *and her* HUSBAND *leave]*

I suppose you know, Adam, that Andrew has died?

ADAM

Podczaski? My old friend from the time of the uprising.

STANISLAW

Well, we expected it. Andrew had to be killed in the end by that consumption of his.

ADAM

I remember the crossing on the Pilica . . . how we hurried to get to the edge of the forest. . . . That was when they smashed my leg.[5]

5. The Pilica is a river in central Poland, a tributary of the Vistula. Adam Chmielowski was wounded in the right leg by an artillery shell while riding with dispatches on 30 September 1863 at the battle of Melchów. His horse was killed under him and he himself had to be abandoned in a peasant cottage by retreating Polish forces. His leg was amputated below the knee by a Russian army surgeon.

LUCIAN

For that matter, Adam, you should take better care of yourself. Death is obstinate about haunting old insurgents. You're not as strong as you used to be in those days. And then you roam about until late at night, without food, God knows where. That won't improve your health. Elizabeth worries about you.

ADAM

Oh, thank you. Your house has been like a home to me.

LUCIAN

Come to visit us soon, won't you? We haven't seen you for so long. You could come with Stanislaw.

And now we must go. Stanislaw, you wanted me to do something for you at the union. We can go there now.

STANISLAW

Very well. See you tomorrow, Adam.

MAX

That goes for me too.

[They all leave. A moment's silence. Only the STRANGER *has stayed behind. Seemingly uninvolved in the conversation, he has moved slowly from one painting to another, with the expression of a connoisseur]*

STRANGER

Well, now we can talk about our business.

ADAM

Forgive me for making you wait so long.

STRANGER

It suited me very well. I was able to complete my analysis.

ADAM

Analysis?

STRANGER

Yes. Allow me to refer to the conversation I have just witnessed here. It is not polite to listen to a conversation in which one does not take part, but my life's mission is largely based on listening in. Yours too.

ADAM

I do not think so.

STRANGER

You mean, unlike me you do not listen in on other people's conversations. Even so, you live by listening in. I've often wondered how you could overhear so many truths even though you lead such a distracting life. You're a big puzzle to me—I must say that right away.

ADAM

I don't understand what you have in mind. But first, about this business of overhearing conversations—assuming that you do listen in on them—I know you have overheard one. It was difficult for you not to do so since those who were talking did not lower their voices in your presence. So they risked being overheard, and I don't think they minded. Do you know any of them?

STRANGER

Yes, by name almost all; they are famous people. But I don't know any of them personally. I've never moved in those circles and listened to what is said . . .

ADAM

So they are themselves to blame.

STRANGER

And now permit me to give my opinion. To you I shall say what I think. I renounce the right to hide my thoughts. I do this not out of sentiment but simply because it fits in with my plans for you.

ADAM

Which means? . . .

STRANGER

It will be amusing to prove how wrong all these people are about you. I repeat, we are entering the range of my plans. I must know where others are wrong in order to avoid their errors. At stake here is a cause that goes far beyond their common concern. *[Pause]*

I don't know what it was about you that worried the priest. I think his misjudgment of you was quite impersonal . . . Your other friends want at any price to reduce your anger to an outburst of artistic genius.

Yes, your anger is what matters. This anger is precious, invaluable. This anger is your way of overhearing things; it is your intuition, your way of sensing what the masses feel. *[Pause]* Yes, Adam. The masses feel an immense, boundless anger. For the moment, it lurks, suspended from the creaking structure of the old order, but not for long. It cannot lurk much longer. This is my view, the result of long and arduous listening. I've told you I live this way. I know the docks of our ports, the mine shafts, and the factory shop floors.

Yes sir, this anger is just. What matters is that it should finally break out, that a universal, almost superhuman force should tear it out of the rotting structures on which for the moment it hangs. *[Pause]* This force is gathering, too. What is it to achieve? I value highly the immense act of collective awareness that is growing. That act has to be speeded up, completed. That act is a vision far more splendid than—you will forgive me—any vision that a painter may have. *[Pause]* And so one must speed up this act of collective awareness. Do you realize what that means? What possibilities for creative work come into view? For that one needs anger. And the feeling for anger. One has to listen. You have that anger and that feeling. You have it by intuition, by talent, by genius. *[Pause]*

ADAM *[Finds words with great difficulty]*

I don't know . . . If you're not mistaken in your view . . . I do not know . . . It seems to me you are wrong . . .

STRANGER

Of course, it's inevitable that you should resist at first. You must cross a threshold. You are not yet sufficiently aware of your own anger. *[Laughs]* A holy simpleton who does not know his own genius. Yes, that's how it was in the old days. Our times require a different inspiration. Dialectics of history, you know. But no matter—

Yes, yes. This is the first resistance that must be broken.

ADAM

And you hope to break it?

STRANGER

I want to shape this splendid material in you. I feel committed to doing this. It is the logical outcome of my plans.

ADAM

Well, so many forces are struggling within me. You too can try.

STRANGER

First, I want to rebuke you for your pictures. That is not the way . . .

ADAM

Ah . . .

STRANGER

That is not the way to express the anger you feel. That is not the way to concentrate your strength. You dissipate it on sentiment, on moods. You want to run away from your own anger to your experiences, to corners of the so-called soul.

Sir, this anger has an objective value. It must not be dissipated. You are responsible for every particle of collective awareness, determining whether it will mature now or later . . .

ADAM

I have never heard such a view . . .

STRANGER

Because no one has looked below the surface. No one has been able to have such insight and such perspective.

[Knock on the door]

ADAM

Come in. *[A few beggars enter]* Ah, it's you. Good, good. Go there, to that room. Everything's ready.

Have you eaten? No? It's all right. I'll bring you something right away.

*[*ADAM *leads them inside, returns. Pause]*

STRANGER

I rebuke you for this as well, for dissipating your strength. This could suffice on the lower levels of collective awareness. No, I've put it wrong: it serves to harness that awareness, not allowing it to mature earlier and erupt.

ADAM *[Interrupting softly]*

"The poor always ye have with you . . ."

STRANGER

Now, when collective awareness has matured in anger, it will deal with that too.

ADAM

But if that is the truth . . .

STRANGER

Then it is necessary to find the point of distortion. If it is the truth, it has certainly been distorted.

ADAM *[In a hollow, deeply depressed voice]*

"The poor always ye have with you . . . But me ye have not always . . ."

STRANGER

But what of it, what of it? Ah, charity. A złoty here, a złoty there, for the right to secure the possession of the millions invested in banks. forests, land, bonds, shares . . . who knows what else. This is what it boils down to in practice. For a złoty here, a złoty there, marked and accounted for exactly—while at the same time others toil animal-like, ten, twelve, sixteen hours a day for a miserable penny, for less than the right to live, for the hope of a dubious consolation up above, a consolation that changes nothing but has for centuries fettered the mighty, magnificent eruption of human anger—creative human anger.

ADAM *[Puts his head in his hands]*

Is it possible that you may be right in so much that you have said? . . . *[He sinks down onto a bench]* "The poor always ye have . . . me ye have not always . . ." But you know, all that is terrible, terrible!

II. In the Vaults of Anger

[Divergent thoughts break in on Adam from all sides. The faces he meets shine through him, exerting on him the pressure of the words he hears. They transform Adam, in their different ways, but constantly. Sometimes one has an overwhelming impression that they create him. But in flashes we realize suddenly with the utmost certainty that he, Adam, creates himself out of them. He constantly creates. After all, he wants to balance the immense shocks, the almost superhuman tremors. This is why Adam's toils will be great. And everything that will now happen, though it will happen around him, will become in him. We move always along the edge where the throbbing pulse of wavering faces and thoughts and words connects with Adam's soul and sets in motion a new discovery of his own "self," recreating and transforming him.

The new Adam emerges gradually and is revealed amid the trepidation and fear of the old Adam. The very need to change, and particularly the course of that change, constitutes the mainspring of the dramatic tension. It is not, however, the tension of two opposite objects, but a full tension within the one object. For at any given moment Adam exchanges some part of his old self for some part of a new one. Gain and progress result from this exchange, but also pain. Here is the living tissue of Adam's drama. People and objects unite in him, changed with an obstinate force from within, accepted or rejected, won and lost, found and forgotten. And in the process, he is revealed to himself, constantly astonished at his own fate. It must be so, because thanks to that astonishment he reveals in himself the love that works through him.

Such is the space in which this chapter of Adam's story takes place. Let us not look for definite places where its particular parts take place. They all become either a subject of recollection, or imagination, or thought, or love, unconnected with any unity of place other than the unity of psychological space.]

1

[About the municipal poorhouse one does not have to think at all or know anything. But he who has come to know it as well as Adam can easily reconstruct for himself what goes on in it on a very cold January evening. And in reconstructing it, he will not just be left to his memory or imagination but will indeed be among those with whom his fate is more and more deeply bound. No matter that he is now walking down a nearby street. His thoughts are with them. He is afraid to face them once more but feels that he must. The distance between him and them narrows rapidly. It will suffice to try the door. The worthless lock will yield easily. And then all those people will be present before him. Just now, though, they are only a jumble of voices.]

VOICE

If the council don't give us more coal in this freezing cold, we'll go smash the mayor's windows!

VOICE

Yeah. And those of the welfare people.

VOICE

Let them see how their teeth chatter from the cold!

VOICE *[Resigned]*

You'll get nowhere. They'll call glaziers and replace them.

VOICE *[Determined]*

Then we'll smash all the glass in their workshops.

VOICE

Shut up! You've become a beggar, so try to behave like one.

VOICE *[Jeers]*

After all, you have a comfy life—no duties, no responsibility. You can live like a philosopher, carry all your possessions in your pocket, and reflect on the vanity of all that's not yours.

VOICE *[Wailing]*

If only the soup were better. It's just water and an odd potato. It's hard to stand out there in the cold after such "refreshment."

VOICE

Not worth hanging around for the soup!

VOICE *[Jeers again]*

No whining now. What do you want? You get up at nine, rested, refreshed. Then you put on your fur coat—oh yes!—and stand like a dignitary for a few hours in one of the main streets, so that anyone who wants can see you and enjoy your company at will. And so that you can watch other people rush in a frenzy to and fro. And you? You are carefree and unconcerned. Then you get your soup. You go home—well, you come here. In the evening you can read the newspaper, if the lamp doesn't smoke. What more do you want? You live like a philosopher.

[Another voice confides sadly to his neighbor]

VOICE

I can't find any work, no matter how hard I try. I've been everywhere. And every night it's back to the poorhouse. I'm sick and tired of the "comfort" here. Occasionally they let me deliver a package, so I don't starve to death. But even then I have to watch out or the regular messengers kick me out.

VOICE *[Advising him]*

You could try coming with us. Short hours, responsibility, though the job's a bit nerve-racking. If it goes well, you can wave good-bye to the poorhouse for a few lovely months and even move into the Europejski Hotel. If things go wrong, you come back to the poorhouse, or worse. What of it? It's a rich, varied life. You just have to know how to go about living it.

VOICE

No, no. He'd better not try with us. He's too stupid for our work.

VOICE

He wants to earn his keep. One of those who would slave like a mule. That's not the way.

VOICE

Is it our fault that some are rich and some are poor?

[From another direction]

VOICE

Put some coal on the fire! Straw alone won't warm our bones.

VOICE

Coal? There isn't any.

VOICE

They're mean, that's what. Other people have so much coal they don't know what to do with it!

VOICE

It's your own fault. You've used up the coal too fast, so now let your teeth chatter!

VOICE

No way to warm yourself up, inside or outside.

VOICE

You'd prefer inside, eh?

VOICE

Who wouldn't? *[After a while]* What's inside is better for a man. Just a few drops . . .

VOICE

Oh yes? What strange fancies you've got.

*[*ADAM *is now among them. The moment of his entry is not important; he has been with them for some time. Everything that has happened among them has happened within him too. But now that the door has yielded easily, notwithstanding the cold,* ADAM'S *eyes have acquired the image that up to now existed stubbornly in his memory and imagination. His inner image—the interior of the poorhouse.* ADAM *is neatly dressed in black and wears a wide-brimmed painter's hat and dark tie. He is dragging with him some sacks or bags. He has approached the nearest group. From now on* ADAM'S *inner space, open to these people, swells with them. Reality]*

ADAM

Excuse me. Maybe you remember me . . . One night Providence made me step into your shelter from the wind and rain . . . Brethren, ever since then some force has urged me to return. I could not do otherwise. Your misery, hunger, homelessness have followed me everywhere . . . *[Silence, indicating indifference]* I didn't know how to return. I looked for ways, for means. Today, for the first time . . .

VOICE *[One of those nearest to him]*

What do you want? If you have nowhere to lie down tonight, go ahead. There's room. No one chases anyone away. It's nobody's property; it's the city's. But hurry; others may come. In such cold no one wants to walk the streets.

VOICE

Are you drunk, brother? What you say doesn't seem to make much sense.

ADAM

You don't understand. I haven't come to live in the poorhouse.

VOICE

No? Then beat it. If you haven't come to live here, what do you want?

VOICE

We pay attention only to those who live here. The rest are trash.

ADAM

But no, no. I've brought you some food and clothes. Given by good people.

VOICE

Ah, benefactors. And you're a benefactor. That's different.

*[*ADAM *begins to empty his bags and sacks onto the nearest bunk. Its occupant gives him a wry look]*

VOICE

What's that?

ADAM

It's for you.

VOICE

For whom? "For you," indeed. They'll be at one another's throats.

*[*VOICES *shout all over the stage]*

VOICE

I want it!

VOICE

Here, this coat, it's for me!

VOICE

I want bread. I haven't eaten since morning!

VOICE

I wouldn't mind having a bite!

VOICE

And a drink!

VOICE *[Angry]*

Good people! Benefactors!

VOICE *[From a corner]*

What's the noise all about?

VOICE

Shut up. They've brought some grub and rags.

VOICE

Who has?

VOICE

Someone! Looks like a nut.

VOICE

From whom?

VOICE

From benefactors.

VOICE

We don't need it!

VOICE

From those whose windows you wanted to smash.

VOICE

I did and I do. They stuff themselves, keep warm, and then when they've worn out their clothes and patched them in ten places, they give them to a beggar. Benefactors, indeed! . . .

[A YOUNG MAN *has approached* ADAM*]*

YOUNG MAN

Would you know of any work, sir?

ADAM

Possibly. Could you come and see me tomorrow?

YOUNG MAN

Where?

ADAM

One Basztowa Street.

YOUNG MAN

I'll come in the morning.

ADAM

Very well.

VOICE *[In the corner, emphatically]*

Eh, you! Listen, you benefactor, take this stuff and beat it!

VOICE *[Close to* ADAM*, softly]*

You know, sir, they get mad here at anyone who is well dressed and not hungry.

VOICE

The council should take better care of us!

VOICE

You wouldn't happen to have a tiny piece of jewelry on you?

VOICE

Shut up!

VOICE *[From the corner, obstinately]*

Well, do you hear me? Beat it, I say, or I'll get up and throw you out.

VOICE *[Near]*

Sir, I could use a coat.

ADAM

I'll do my best next time.

VOICE

Who knows when that'll be!

VOICE

Next winter, when you're dead and buried.

VOICE *[The* MAN *in the corner stands up]*

I'm telling you for the last time. All of you are scum! If someone spits in your face, you'll take it. Those scoundrels in their warm, comfy palaces wear fancy clothes, drink liqueurs; and sometimes, if they feel like it, they throw you a scrap: an old rag or moldy bread. And you bow to them, call them benefactors, and kiss their hands.

It's all unjust. It's wrong. Don't you get it?

Why is he wearing a suit and tie while I have nothing to put on my back? Enough, enough. He should make himself scarce.

[Murmuring in the corner. ADAM *lowers his eyes, keeps silent like a man who has been whipped. He takes everything they say personally]*

VOICE

Better to spit on them, as they have spit on you.

[People have collected the things ADAM *has brought and are trying them on. The* MAN *in the corner has jumped onto the middle bunk]*

MAN

Don't dare touch it! Understand? Or I'll kill you! *[Some of the others surround him, forming a wall]* Don't you understand? Let him take it all back. That's worth more than these rags.

VOICES

Shut up! We're not giving it back!

[The MAN *begins to beat right and left with a stick]*

MAN

You riffraff! Stupid beggars!

[The others duck. One of them tries to push him off the bunk. They grab him by the legs]

VOICE

Eh, watch it, we can get you too!

[Someone has grabbed the end of his stick. The two men struggle. ADAM *looks horrified. He tries to say something. His hands fall limp]*

ADAM

Brothers, brothers. You've misunderstood me. *[Louder]* You've misunderstood me!

VOICE *[Above his head]*

Away with you! Go!

*[*ADAM *moves away, leaving everything in turmoil. Now he is alone, but he carries within him the full picture of that struggle and turmoil. He hears the heartbeats, feels the dull pressure at the top of his head. The pain of his dilemma has deepened in the feeling of helplessness]*

2

[The light of a nearby street lamp clearly separates ADAM'S *shadow from his figure. He feels this shadow as an actual presence of some-one strange. He senses that he is not alone. Between him and the "stranger made present" a dialogue ensues that takes place in an atmosphere of tense concentration. It is not clear whether he has a dialogue with himself or with someone else.]*

THE OTHER

It is not easy to distinguish between one's own thoughts and those that come from without.

ADAM

Which means . . .

THE OTHER

Which means that in a certain situation one ought to recognize certain impulses as one's own, and not seek their cause outside oneself.

ADAM

Can someone else apply his thoughts so tightly to one's brain as to conceal the gap between the mind and the imputed thought? The gap or the break . . .

THE OTHER

I assure you he can't. Your reasoning is absolutely right.

ADAM

Where does it lead?

THE OTHER

To not overrating your own strength.

ADAM

Where?

THE OTHER

To rejecting reckless undertakings!

ADAM

Where else?

THE OTHER

To retreat! You see, all this makes sense only up to a point. What can you do about ill will or stubbornness? They remain what they want to remain. That won't be your fault.

ADAM

Your reasoning is absolutely correct.

THE OTHER

I see I am dealing with a sensible man, who won't attempt the impossible . . .

ADAM

Thanks to correct reasoning like yours, we sink more and more. But wait: how can it be " like yours?" I really don't know: "yours" or "mine." But if "yours," then whose? There is no one here.

[But in the background there is a man, limp, leaning against a lamp-post]

THE OTHER

Well, of course. Don't concern yourself about him. Think: I am not the world's buttress. I am an intelligence, whose entire task is to reveal the true image of the world and not care for the rest.

Think thus! You too are an intelligence. That means you are subject to the laws of intelligence. It is enough to hold the image of the world in your thoughts. You have no obligation to put its heavy burden on your back. You are too tired.

ADAM

I really don't know if these thoughts are my own or if someone prompts them in me.

THE OTHER

I don't want to be severe with you. Remain yourself. Finish the canvases you've begun. Then—arrange an exhibition. What else can you do? Indeed, I advise you never to return to the poorhouse, unless you want to do harm . . .

ADAM

To what?

THE OTHER

To the liberation of those people. This must wait. It must be accomplished slowly, from within. It must grow and mature on its own among them. You no doubt wish to take there things that are strange to them.

ADAM

For instance?

THE OTHER

For instance, you would have them pray, isn't that so? Work, carry the so-called cross?

ADAM

Well?

THE OTHER

You see, that is not what they need. They must be given human maturity.

ADAM

Oh, you have the capacity to produce your thoughts strangely alongside mine. Again I cannot distinguish anything . . . Well then . . . human maturity—what does that mean?

THE OTHER

That means, maturity dictated by the conditions of their existence.

ADAM

You still try to avoid certain points, though. That is beginning to surprise me.

THE OTHER

Because you are a madman, and I must have the sense, the moderation you lack.

ADAM

Again I might think that you are me.

THE OTHER

But of course.

ADAM

Could I be split into you and the one in me who keeps rising and asking for more? . . .

THE OTHER

Not at all. I am only a factor in the equilibrium of your self . . .

[They walk past the man leaning limply against a lamppost]

ADAM

The self that now demands that I ask this man *[He speaks aloud]*, Why are you standing here?

THE OTHER

Quiet! Don't wake him.

ADAM

Wake him? He is clearly emaciated and that's why . . . *[Does not finish the sentence]* And then, there is something more in him than just a beggar leaning against a lamppost.

THE OTHER

Really? I don't know anything about it.

ADAM

Exactly. There is an image.

THE OTHER

Ah yes, for you everything has value as an image. You are a painter.

ADAM

A nonpictorial image. An image that is imperceptible to my eye but that preys on my soul.

THE OTHER

Don't give in. Leave it. Forget.

ADAM *[As if not having heard]*

Image and likeness.

THE OTHER

Likeness? Whose?

ADAM

You don't know! So there is a sphere in my thought that you do not possess. Which means that you do not grow out of my mind like my own thoughts. Ah, I have exposed you. I have done so with this image and likeness you do not want to know; . . . though you do know . . .

Ah, wait—likeness and image. You see—he is a child; he is a son. I too. You . . .

THE OTHER

Not I. Never.

ADAM

No? Then the great mirror of the world reflects only the void in you, the dull, dark void of your existence.

THE OTHER

I've told you I am an intelligence. That is enough for me. For you too.

ADAM

You try to persuade me. But facts are against you. Oh, do you see that man leaning against the lamppost?

THE OTHER

He does not attract my intelligence. He has ceased to be an issue for me. I can go past him.

ADAM

Oh, how much is missing in you, how much you miss!

[On the other side of ADAM *the even, unbroken darkness of the street expands.* ADAM *has passed the place where the street lamp had cast the shadow.* THE OTHER *is no more.* ADAM *lifts the tramp, supporting him with his arm. He drags the man, who limps on his right leg]*

Come, my friend. You're not saying anything? Your hands . . . oh, you're freezing . . . You cannot walk . . . Well, come! *[*ADAM *almost carries him on his back]* Come. You have saved me.

3

*[*ADAM *with the painting of a man who is Christ: "Ecce Homo." Is this the picture that had to grow in his soul after he had been to see the forsaken ones? The fate of the picture and the fate of man.* ADAM'S *implements for painting are lying on the floor. The action again takes place within him.]*

ADAM

You are always deeper than my vision. And always distant. I cannot extract you from my sense of sight. That means—wait—that means . . .

Is what I carry in my field of vision, and what I embrace with my soul, not in accord with You any more?

My vision is silent.

Ecce Homo by Adam Chmielowski, 1879-1881

Why? Why? Tell me, what else is there that I can do for You in them?

How can I ask You about it, You who knew no bounds! But I, I keep searching for the line of what I can embrace without drawing any contours, and for the imprint of what I carry in me without feeling the burden.

Thus the burden I impress and the contour I draw are not Your outline or the imprint of Your beauty.

They are!

How much confidence is required here, how much change of vision! I beg You: alter my sight!

I can do nothing more. Nothing. Besides, they do not need me. That is clear. Tell me how to extricate myself. They don't need me. Yes, I've found that out. I am convinced of it. Why can't I convince You?

Tell me Yourself, what will remain of me, of what use shall I be, if You reject my painting and they reject me? *[Pause]*

Ah . . . Ah. Again You are above my thoughts. You speak in them—silence, hush . . . This moment is awesome and wondrous. Quiet . . . hush . . . hush . . . hush.

So many people in the world have been unable to face up to this moment; its enchantment overwhelmed their weakness. Shall I be equal to it?

Well then, yes, yes . . . I shall be worthy of that dispossession; I shall gain as much as I lose, as much as I leave behind, rid myself of. Yes, yes.—Yes, yes.

But tell me—can You ask that of a man? Can You ask that of me? How can I cease to be who I am?

*[*ADAM *resumes work for a little while, passionately, feverishly. As he works, he speaks]*

You must take this form for me, the form that I embrace with my soul and these patches of color on canvas, and You in so many people—are one . . . *[With effort]*

Are one!

[He takes a step back]

This is how I will preserve You in so many, many people. *[He takes another step back]*

What's wrong with that?

Can this be against You? *[He steps still farther back]*

No. No.

[A turning point]

Bu this is not You.

You are alien.

You are distant.

You are more and more alien to the one I know.

My vision of You is fading, but at the same time I see You more and more clearly.

How can this be?

[Again he looks intently at the picture]

But it is not You.

So it's not true that I preserve You in so many people, in so many souls.

[He puts aside his palette and brushes. He approaches the window, looks at the Vistula River. Someone has come in]

VOICE

You're looking away again. You're not painting.

*[*ADAM *does not turn his head]*

ADAM

Is that you, Max?

4
Adam's Confession

[The confessor's face is hidden by his hands. One can only guess where in the shadow his eyes are shining. Or maybe they are closed now. The two shapes are hardly noticeable in the dusk, which blends strangely with the whisper of their words.]

PRIEST

What else have you to confess, my son? *[*ADAM *remains silent]* Maybe you are beset by temptations or anxieties?

ADAM

Yes. My greatest temptation is the thought that one can love with the intelligence, with the intelligence only, and that this will suffice.

PRIEST

What do you mean?

ADAM

I see in such love the only possible release from all these matters that I have taken so much of your time with, Father.

PRIEST

Wait a moment, my brother. There is too much resignation in what you have just said. I would accept that but for the feeling that there is even more anxiety in it.

ADAM

How is that, Father? I know they don't need me, and at the same time God does not need my art.

PRIEST

You are wrong, my brother. They do need you, and God regards your art with a father's eye. After all, it brings people nearer to Him. You attempt to search for His glory through it.

ADAM

Exactly. Tell me, Father, how can that be? I have a deep conviction that it is so—yet, something underneath destroys that belief.

What remains of us then? What remains of us before God? Only rejection, I suppose?

PRIEST

Indeed. Nothing remains of us then. Of ourselves nothing remains. But then, just then, what remains in us is simply His grace.

ADAM

Is not His grace bound up with the feeling that we are His sons? Can that grace persist in us as an awareness of having been dispossessed?

PRIEST

Yes. That would indeed seem improbable but for one fact. You know, my brother: "My God, my God, why hast thou forsaken me?" "Father, all things are possible to thee; let this cup pass from me . . ." Yet He was not just an adopted Son.

[A moment's silence, as if he is searching for the right word]

And he spoke those words precisely at a time when He was adopting anew the rejected sons. It was just such a moment.

ADAM

But I can't. I am not able to. If they do not need me at all, if there is no logical reason for my being among them . . . if I simply cannot remain among them as myself . . . then how, how can I be an instrument for their adoption as sons? . . .

PRIEST

These things do not follow directly from one another. Who knows whether their rejecting you would not have the greatest significance—

ADAM

But in that case they would take away my right to be an artist.

PRIEST

Not quite.

ADAM

But Father, try to understand. I cannot love two different things, for I cannot love by halves. I cannot remain half way between the two chasms that draw me.

PRIEST

Why do you look at it like that? One can love God in many ways.

ADAM

Everybody says so. Why then does this universally accepted truth not ring true to me?

PRIEST

I don't know. Souls have their different ways, different courses of purification.

ADAM

Ah yes. I began to find dirt in what used to be an ideal.

PRIEST

Perhaps. A mission requires purification.

ADAM

What will you say to me, Father?

PRIEST

Let yourself be molded by love.

ADAM

How?

PRIEST

I don't know. Your love is your own, your asset. I cannot judge your love by its tiniest throbs.

ADAM

But if you were to weigh command and prohibition, rejection and acceptance . . .

PRIEST

These matters are too great, too important. Where love is concerned, one cannot give orders. Just think. Our Lord accomplishes so much through love, so much good. Love joins us with Him more than anything else because it transforms everything.

[Again he remains silent for a while, as if he cannot find the right expression. He finds it in the end and adds very quietly]

Let yourself be molded by love.

*[*ADAM *rises from his knees, takes his hands away from his face, and immediately walks off with a step at first unsure, then firm. He passes many streets, no doubt, walks past many thresholds, lurking beneath his feet. He walks]*

5

[A door opens and he is again surrounded by the familiar crowd who inhabit the poorhouse. One can sense that for ADAM *they have emerged as a tangible reality, tempered by imagination and memory. They have appeared suddenly from the recesses of a long-lasting opposition of heart and will. So they are the same people as before, similarly placed in the dark space. As soon as some of them have noticed* ADAM*, they tell their neighbors.]*

VOICE

Ah, it's him.

VOICE

Still not fed up?

VOICE

He should have had enough . . .

ADAM *[His thought takes up the thread of theirs]*

Yes, I've had enough. He hasn't.

[But that is his last thought. Now come the words. But on the face of it, they begin at a different point from his last thought. And ADAM *speaks them aloud]*

Brothers, will you receive me today? I've managed to collect something for you again.

VOICE

Oh yes, why not?

VOICE

Have you got that coat for me?

VOICE

Did you remember to bring what I asked for?

VOICE

You can safely do as you wish today; Victor isn't here, the one who started that row. Others wouldn't have dared without him. The police have got him now . . .

[Others approach]

VOICE

You must have found some work for Stefan. He doesn't come here any more.

ADAM

Yes, I have.

VOICE

We've nothing against your coming here, sir . . . We realize that society has to take care of us.

VOICE

Right.

VOICE

It's more convenient to take what's brought to you than to go begging. If only there were enough of it. As it is, we have to go stand on street corners anyway.

[They unwrap the sacks and bags ADAM *has brought. A clamor ensues as they try to grab the contents]*

VOICE

I want that sheepskin . . .

VOICE

Really, I've got nothing but holes . . .

VOICE

What do you want? You have old Pawalec's coat.

VOICE

What horrible rags . . .

VOICE

Just look, mates! You couldn't imagine worse tatters.

VOICE

That Victor fellow was right.

VOICE *[To* ADAM*]*

You know, sir, they say Victor was right because he yelled a lot about worn-out rags that some people would throw to the poor. But to tell you the truth, they didn't understand Victor. Frankly, he was concerned with much more. Do you follow me?

ADAM

I do. And I accept that.

VOICE *[To* ADAM*]*

Well then, sir?

ADAM

Well what? I can't abolish everything.

VOICE *[To* ADAM*]*

Would you like to?

ADAM

Others have asked me that too . . .

VOICE *[To* ADAM*]*

And what would you do? . . .

[The scramble around the gifts continues]

VOICE

These shirts must be made of sackcloth.

VOICE

You'd rather have silk, would you?

VOICE

Who wouldn't?

VOICE

He didn't bring much food today, did he?

VOICE

Stop grumbling. Take what there is, and don't be choosy!

VOICE

There's nothing to be choosy about.

VOICE *[To* ADAM, *the same speaker as before]*

And what would you do?

ADAM

I don't know. The rich must give some of their wealth to the poor.

VOICE *[To* ADAM*]*

I'm sick and tired of it: poor, poor . . .

[Around the gifts]

VOICE

I suppose you've had enough of all this charity.

VOICE

I doubt if we'll ever see him here again.

VOICE *[To* ADAM, *the same speaker]*

I'm not sure if you've found the right way. To call someone like Victor or myself "poor" or a "beggar" is like spitting in our faces. We're not beggars by profession. We're victims of the order, the system, if you like.

[Around the gifts, the VOICES *talk to* ADAM*]*

VOICE

Eh, listen sir . . .

VOICE

Yeah, we're very grateful that they think . . .

VOICE

Yes, we've nothing against . . .

VOICE

But if you could tell those benefactors to keep some of these rags for themselves. A beggar doesn't necessarily have to wear tatters.

VOICE

[The same speaker who talked to ADAM *now talks to the others]*

Then why do you call yourselves beggars?

VOICE

What should we call ourselves?

VOICE

It's as if you took someone by the throat.

VOICE

Why not call things by their names?

VOICE

If you're such a gentleman, go, scram.

VOICE

Like Victor.

VOICE

You're stupid! You're all stupid.

VOICE

And you're a wiseguy.

VOICE

You've gotten used to beggars' ways, so you call yourselves beggars.

VOICE

And how about you?

VOICE

Not I! I'll fight for my rights!

VOICE

They'll get you just as they did Victor.

VOICE

Victor was a villain. He deserved to be caught.

VOICE

And you're not a villain? They'll find a law for you too.

*[*ADAM *watches all this, wide-eyed]*

VOICE

I've tried to convince this gentleman here.

VOICE

What can he do? He can only bring what he gets. He's not rich himself.

VOICE

No, he isn't. I know it well, for I've slept at his place.

VOICE

Oh! He puts people up, does he?

VOICE

Oh yes, he takes any old tramp.

VOICE

Well, well . . . What is he?

VOICE

You'd never guess.

VOICE

A civil servant or a teacher.

VOICE

No. Guess—he's a painter.

VOICE

Oh!

[Their conversation flags]

VOICE *[The same speaker who talked to* ADAM *before]*
Tell us what you think about it all. The fact that you sometimes bring us some rags does not . . .

VOICE
They say you're a painter.

[A moment of expectation and slight tension]

ADAM
What do you really want of me?

VOICE
Don't take any notice of these foulmouthed and empty-bellied fools. Show them your finger, and they'll bite your hand.

ADAM
Yes, but it's clear you want something more. I can see that.

VOICE
Well, if you could give us more to eat and better rags.

ADAM
Yes, yes. But you want something more. He wants something more *[Points to the man who has been talking to him],* and he . . . and he . . .

I know. What you want is just, most just. That's it. That's what matters, and it matters that you should want it. Not to consider yourselves outcasts, but to get out of this quagmire.

Yes, it's just and proper.

[A sudden outburst]

But why do you want it from me? It's too much. It's too much.

WOMAN'S VOICE
What is it, sir? We don't want anything new from you. Bring us what you can, what they give you . . . It's all right.

ADAM

No . . . I mean yes, you don't want anything else, but He . . . One word was enough. One of you spoke one word, one sentence . . . and that was enough . . . I know He wants it . . .

ANOTHER WOMAN'S VOICE

What are you dreaming about? Who's he?

ADAM

Because I— it is true—I wanted to redeem myself . . . give a coat here, a loaf of bread there, put someone up . . . But none of this means anything . . . beggars, tramps, street urchins still remain . . .

VOICE

We've had enough of this!

ADAM

Yes. We've had enough of this.

VOICE *[The same one who spoke earlier]*

I see you took my meaning.

VOICE

What does it matter, as long as we get some more rags—

VOICE

And bread that's whiter—

VOICE

And something to drink.

ADAM *[His thoughts clarify; he has a revelation]*

Brothers are to rise!

VOICE *[The same one who talked to him before]*

You think so? Hm. What of it? We've heard such words before.

ADAM *[Even more strength in his voice]*

There are to be brothers!

VOICE

Forget it. The main thing is to get some rags sometimes—

VOICE

Not too tattered—

VOICE

And some meat—

VOICE

And vodka—

ADAM

No, no! Enough!

VOICE *[The same one who talked to him before]*

Shut up! Stop your beggars' whining!

ADAM

What matters is that a man
such as I
who has become the son . . .

*[*ADAM *leaves suddenly. The people call after him]*

VOICE

Don't forget next time.

VOICE

Eh, a shirt for me—

VOICE

And for me a . . .

VOICE

Quiet, can't you see he's gone?

VOICE

Ah!

VOICE

Eh, sir!

VOICE *[The one who talked to* ADAM*]*

Shut up . . . What matters is that a man . . . *[After a while]* Shut up! . . . Don't you see what's happened to him?

VOICES

What?

6

[When ADAM *walks quickly past the same street lamp as before, his shadow is suddenly torn away and cast upon the pale wall of the nearest building. The impression is an eerie one.* ADAM *slows his pace and stops, lost in thought. But whom are we to expect beyond the edge of* ADAM'S *persistent thoughts? Just an irritated alter ego, angrily implicated in their course? Or does the alter ego itself constitute a response to their passage upward, their lifting up?]*

THE OTHER

You are stubborn, after all.

ADAM

Someone is speaking beside me.

THE OTHER

You are stubborn. Your obstinacy will break you. You'll see.

[ADAM does not turn his head, but guided by a subconscious feeling, he conducts the whole conversation as if talking over his shoulder]

ADAM

And the worst of it is that again I cannot distinguish between myself and the one who speaks.

THE OTHER

Of course, because the intelligence has been enhanced.

ADAM

Oh no, you're wrong.

THE OTHER

You've put it badly. Don't say, "You're wrong" but simply, "I am wrong."

ADAM

Well then: I am wrong . . . *[A sudden flash]* Oh no, last time you succeeded in reducing the matter to the limits of knowledge. You will not make that mistake again today.

THE OTHER

You keep using the wrong person.

ADAM

Today you will not make that mistake again.

THE OTHER

Why not?

ADAM

Because you will not be able to reduce everything to the limits of intelligence.

THE OTHER

Ho, ho . . . Why ever not?

ADAM

Because I am letting myself be molded by love.

THE OTHER

Exactly. Exactly. One can see it at once. There is nothing that would do so much harm to knowledge.

Do you understand? You call it love. But for me it is only an unbearable burden, an unbearable strain on knowledge, a destruction of knowledge, a watering down of knowledge, a distortion of knowledge, a warping of knowledge.

Do you understand? It is the cancellation of knowledge.

And that is why you and others like you cannot share my knowledge, because you have distorted it, desecrated it, defiled it.

You see now? And you call it love.

This you call love.

[From now on the vision is blurred, incoherent, unreal, removed from truth]

You can't get out of this mess, of course!

ADAM

Ah, you've nearly hit the mark.

THE OTHER

You feel it, yes? And you—this goes also for others like you—call it love: that blurring of the picture, getting it wrong, destroying the picture . . .

Burning the picture!

ADAM

Am I to consider this a temptation?

[I do not know whether it is true that ADAM *burned some of his paintings to free himself for Christ in the poor]*

THE OTHER

For a long time now you have been tempting yourself and the whole complex of forces that surpass you.

ADAM

I know one Force in particular that surpasses me. It surpasses me infinitely in love. I cannot bear that strain. This shames and humiliates me, but it also guides me, lets me develop . . .

THE OTHER

Oh, unhappy man, how far you have departed from clarity of thought!

*[*ADAM *gives a long loud laugh]*

THE OTHER

Why do you laugh? *[*ADAM *goes on laughing. His laugh is bright and sincere, like that of a young boy.* ADAM *has not laughed like this for a long time. Resistance to his laughter can be felt from his shadow. From it too can be heard an uncanny echo of that sincere laugh]* Well? Why do you laugh like one of those idiots with whom you insist on mixing? Similis simili! . . .

ADAM

Maybe . . . Right now I am simply overjoyed at the thought that someone as helpless as I, clumsy and lame, can rid himself of undeniable intelligence, can possess something that bypasses it,

something that exposes it,
unmasks it,
betrays it.

THE OTHER

I repeat: You've just been in a circle of idiots!

ADAM

Maybe. For the price I've paid, I've also freed myself from the tyranny of intelligence.

THE OTHER

You have given up a clear image of the world.

ADAM

I have found an image you don't know about.

THE OTHER

So?

ADAM

So you will not be able to go on pretending that you are me, that you and I are the same.

You are different, infinitely different.

7

[After all that has happened, ADAM *is tired. He does not work, does not go out for days. You can find him sitting wearily in his high-backed chair. No wonder he is fatigued, for that strange death that is the beginning of life has overcome him. Do not be surprised, Marynia—*MARYNIA *is* ADAM'S *sister, who has just come from the country, disturbed by his condition—do not be surprised all of you who now visit* ADAM *less frequently, frightened by his apparent strangeness. Because* ADAM'S *friends come less often,* MARYNIA *often remains in the studio alone with her brother. She tries to find out what ails him and, in her woman's way, looks for familiar remedies.]*

MARYNIA

I think, Adaś, that you should come to us and have a rest.

ADAM

From what?

MARYNIA

From pictures, from the abundance of pictures.

ADAM

My friends say I don't do anything . . . Max says so . . . Well, maybe . . . Maybe I could have a rest.

MARYNIA

Indeed, Adaś, our Podolian fields would do you good . . . Remember how the field, a field of the richest wheat, breaks off suddenly . . . and a gorge opens, the river down below. The water is dear and bright. The people are simple . . .

ADAM

Yes, one could . . .

MARYNIA

You could break away, revive your spirits.

ADAM

One could . . . help those people too . . . but the poverty here is more acute.

MARYNIA

I want to help *you,* Adaś. They've written to me that you are ill . . .

ADAM

It depends.

*[*UNCLE JOSEPH *enters]*

UNCLE JOSEPH

Ah, Adam . . .

ADAM

Uncle . . .

MARYNIA

How good of you to come, Uncle. I am trying to persuade Adaś to spend some time with us at Kudryńce.[6]

UNCLE JOSEPH

That would be wonderful, Adam, wonderful. You would see my orphanage.

ADAM

Oh yes?

UNCLE JOSEPH

That's right. Peasant children, orphans. It has revealed to me the purpose of my life. It couldn't have been otherwise. Everything else failed me. But these children have grown attached to me as to their father.

You see, Adaś, we have to go down to them. It's high time for equality. We're guilty of such negligence . . .

ADAM

Indeed, though I have a somewhat different approach . . .

UNCLE JOSEPH

Why, of course, Adaś. I know you are a painter.

ADAM

No, I don't mean that . . . For instance, what do you think about the purpose of such initiatives as yours, Uncle?

UNCLE JOSEPH

What do you want? One does some good. The poor creatures are happy—and so am I . . . A man frees himself from a burden, from the heavy burden of responsibility. All that goes back a long time. Today you have qualms of conscience . . .

---

6. Kudryńce is a village in Podolia on the river Zbrucz in southeastern Poland, where Adam Chmielowski stayed in 1882-1884 with the family of his brother Stanisław. While there he painted a great deal and also engaged in the missionary activity of the Franciscan Third Order.

ADAM

That is true. Yet but for these qualms—

*[*ADAM *has suddenly become harsh.* UNCLE JOSEPH *senses it]*

UNCLE JOSEPH

What do you want? Those are just theories. These qualms are a historic necessity . . .

ADAM *[With the same harsh tone]*

Oh, really?

UNCLE JOSEPH

Social, rather.

ADAM

Well, well . . .

UNCLE JOSEPH

Why do you mock me, my boy? Do you think your pictures can take the place of everything? You don't see the world apart from them. And you think . . .

ADAM

I think something quite opposite. Still, such thinking is no good for anything . . . *[Unexpectedly turns to* MARYNIA*]* Is it true, Marynia, that in Kudryńce people still believe in charity?

MARYNIA

What a strange question.

UNCLE JOSEPH

Precisely. What does it mean?

ADAM

That those people are still primitive in the simplicity of their morals.

UNCLE JOSEPH

Adam, what do you mean by that?

ADAM

Nothing, nothing. You have a very kind heart, Uncle. Surely it would be hard to expect you to fraternize with beggars . . .

UNCLE JOSEPH

What beggars?

ADAM

Ah yes, I forgot; they are children, orphans.

MARYNIA

You are very absentminded, Adaś.

UNCLE JOSEPH

Exactly. Well then? Will you come to Kudryńce?

MARYNIA

He will; most certainly he will.

ADAM

I don't know anything yet.

*[*UNCLE JOSEPH *and* MARYNIA *go out. They do not even take leave of* ADAM. *They must have something to do nearby.*

ADAM, *left alone, sits for a long while, motionless in his chair. Then he wipes his forehead, pushes back his hair. Suddenly he rises. Very slowly he walks to his easels. He passes many of them indifferently before approaching "Ecce Homo." Is not that painting more surely his than the others? He stops in front of it and, in spite of himself, bends down as if stooping under the weight of this subject. He lifts his eyes to the painting. Then he speaks very slowly]*

Still You are terribly unlike Him, whom You are.
You have toiled in every one of them.

You are deadly tired.
They have exhausted You.
This is called Charity.

But with all this You have remained beautiful.
The most beautiful of the sons of men.
Such beauty was never repeated again.
Oh what a difficult beauty, how hard.
Such beauty is called Charity.

[He now turns slowly around and casts his eyes for a while upon the other paintings. Suddenly a smile appears on his lips. Still smiling, he speaks]

Strange—I doubt if any of my Munich friends have tested the accuracy of their painter's vision among the bunks of the poor . . .

And no painter in the world, surely . . .

And yet . . . maybe—

It's a very strange thing.

8
A Collector for Charity

[A street wrapped in darkness. One can hear in the dark a thudding on the pavement, footfalls, regular but intermittent. One cannot see the face of the person walking because the shadow of a tree covers him like a delicate veil. At one point he steps forward a little out of the darkness to meet someone approaching from the other side.]

ADAM

Excuse me.

STRANGER

What is it?

ADAM

Would you like to . . . contribute something for the poor in the municipal poorhouse?

[The STRANGER *looks at him]*

STRANGER

No.

ADAM

Sorry.

*[*ADAM *steps back. The* STRANGER *follows him a few steps]*

STRANGER

I told you a few months ago that this was not the way.

*[*ADAM *raises his eyes only now]*

ADAM

Ah, it's you . . .

STRANGER

This is not the way to do it! This does not strengthen the tremendous collective anger but disarms it, blunts its edge. I explained this to you, remember?

ADAM

Perfectly. I have never really left that conversation behind.

STRANGER

Well, then? Everything I said is right and well founded.

ADAM

Oh no, my friend, oh no . . .

STRANGER

Such an answer only proves to me that you have remained yourself.

You have not abandoned your moods, your complexes; you have not matured into a spokesman.

Do you understand? You have not taken on yourself their strivings, their efforts, their anger; you have not identified yourself with them; you have not lost yourself in them. You understand that.

You have remained yourself, a patron of street and church beggars. You have not transcended yourself. You are not ready for the ideal of free men.

[A moment's silence]

I am disappointed in you. I relied on you to do what's right. I relied on your intelligence. An intelligent and honest man must see these things as I do.

ADAM

It's true. You promised to shape the raw material in me.

STRANGER

But instead, sentiment has prevailed in you. True, I was negligent.

ADAM

Someone else wasn't.

STRANGER

With poor results.

ADAM

One never knows. But on the whole—yes.

STRANGER

Stop lowering your eyes, bending your head like a martyr. I've had enough of it. They too. Do you understand me?

*[*ADAM *remains silent]*

I go on because I feel anger rising in me. I have already told you about your responsibility to the revolution. You let the people down;

you contribute to the disintegration of their powers. And you do it knowingly.

ADAM

Yes. You can be sure that I do it knowingly, with the conviction that it is the only way.

STRANGER

That only increases your guilt.

ADAM

I accept that.

STRANGER

But my only concern is to prove to you that you are wrong. Yes. I will prove it to you at once. Are you willing?

ADAM

Yes, I'm willing. How do you want to do it?

STRANGER

It's very simple. Where is that poorhouse?

ADAM

By the Vistula. Seven Wykręt Street.

STRANGER

Very well. Now, then, we'll both go there at once. It's evening and the people will all be there. I'll talk to them in my own kind of language.

ADAM

Yes.

STRANGER

I am going to tell them about things that have been obscured and impeded in them through your sentimental actions. You will see that out of these doubly depraved people . . . yes, doubly, first by poverty and then by charity—the latter is your doing—I can immediately bring out their human dignity, the proper measure of their humanity and all that just anger of theirs.

ADAM

I accept the conditions.

STRANGER

Let's go, then.

ADAM

Would you mind waiting a while? A large group of people is approaching. This opportunity is too precious for me to miss, you understand. . .

STRANGER

I will go first.

[The STRANGER *disappears into the darkness.* ADAM *steps forward to meet those approaching]*

ADAM

Forgive me. I am a collector for the municipal poorhouse. Would you care to donate something for the poor? . . .

ONE OF THE COMPANY

Who is it?

VOICE

A collector for the poorhouse.

VOICE

But the voice is strangely familiar.

MAX

Adam, is that you?

ADAM

Max—

[A moment's expectant silence. Some embarrassment among those present]

STANISLAW

You see, Adaś, we are escorting Madam Helena home after her premiere.

[ADAM *remains silent]*

GEORGE

A great triumph. Europe has never seen such an Ophelia.

[Silence again]

LUCIAN

How strange your voice sounds in this wilderness, George.

STANISLAW

You're right. There is a wilderness here.

MAX

An immobility.

GEORGE

Stagnation, don't you think?

MAX

Where?

GEORGE

In all of us, no doubt.

[Pause]

LUCIAN

Curious, though. We haven't all met for a long time. The last time—you remember, Adam—was in your studio. That Jesuit was there as well, with his mother. A messenger from the city council came, then a stranger, who didn't say a word to anybody and remained alone with Adam after we'd gone.

GEORGE

I remember. Then Adam disappeared for months.

MAX

Oh no. I know that he was painting *Ecce Homo*, a very interesting picture, foretelling some new technical possibilities. But those were not the most important things about it. Something was twisted about that picture, something not quite up to his potential, yet something that outgrew it. That's as much as I've known about Adam since. But I never supposed that . . .

ADAM *[After a while]*

You never really believed in art, Max.

MAX

I didn't? How's that? Not long ago you said exactly the opposite.

ADAM

And yet . . . You don't believe that a painting is capable of dissecting a man . . . transforming a man.

MAX

Ecce Homo?

*[*ADAM *remains silent]*

LUCIAN

Would you come some of the way with us, Adaś?

ADAM

I can't. I have an important meeting.

LUCIAN

Yes?

ADAM

In a way, the result of everything depends on it . . .

LUCIAN

I have no idea what you mean. But I reproach myself for having lost touch with you recently, and I don't dare to ask directly . . .

ADAM

I mean, my dear fellow, that I am, as you can see, a collector for the municipal poorhouse . . .

LUCIAN

Well?

ADAM

And it might happen that we will go further . . . It largely depends on the meeting I have just mentioned.

LUCIAN

In that case . . . we won't detain you.

GEORGE

Good night.

ADAM

Good night. But don't forget that I am a collector.

*[*MADAM HELENA *approaches with her* HUSBAND. *She takes off her gloves. Without uttering a word she throws into his box the rings she takes from her fingers]*

Thank you. May God reward you.

VOICES

Good night.

9

[Immediately after the company leave, the poorhouse reemerges. In the uniform space of awareness it takes up no less room than all the preceding events. ADAM *hears the quickened pulse in his temples. He has been walking, almost running, the distance to Seven Wykręt Street.*

The light of the only ceiling lamp is even dimmer than before. Some people are sitting or half lying on their bunks, but most of them crowd around the speaker who is standing in their midst.]

STRANGER

What matters is that you have human rights—or let us put it differently: that you have the right to human rights. But you have been denied that right.

VOICE

Who has denied it?

STRANGER

Who?—It is not possible to point to a single culprit. One has to unmask whole groups of people one by one, a whole tangle of abuse and wrongs . . . Of course, no one came here to point a finger at you, or you, and say: You're being deprived of your rights; you have no rights. Nobody has done that. But they have done the same thing by making millions, piling up stocks and shares, showering the world with a heap of paper money that is supported by your work, or your poverty. It is all the same. Work breeds poverty, and poverty serves work. One and the other help them to fortune and affluence. Fortune and affluence! Do you realize what this means?

It is all done to keep you away, you, you, all of you. The screw is tightened, and you are excluded. Of course they will not lift you up, for then the magic ring with which they've squeezed everyone except themselves would break. It is the ring that separates their unbounded freedom from your slavery.

None of you possesses anything—not even that wooden bunk, not even that wisp of straw on which you must lie all night; though it's hard, it's not yours.

But you must understand! Even that is not the worst. The worst is that they want to convince you that none of the little you have is yours by right, that all is given to you out of their generosity, out of charity.

And listen. They yell the same thing at the workers in the factories, at the miners in the mines, at the hired hands on the landed estates. You are born to have nothing, they to have everything.

I have come here to rouse what is dormant in you. I know that just now you all think as I do. You all agree, but no one dares to say so aloud. Why? Why won't you find the strength that is in you? Why do you allow yourselves to be oppressed by poverty and hamper the just rebellion within you? Why is your anger silent?

Do not be afraid!

You need only supply your anger, and forces will emerge that know how to control, use, and direct it!

[There is no response as yet among the people. ADAM *has been present for a while, listening intently]*

Do not expect charity! Charity degrades you. You do not need it. You must realize that all is yours by right, not by charity. Charity is a dismal shadow in which the mysterious rich man tries to hide his real image, wanting at the same time to drown you all in that shadow—your cause, your right, your anger.

Beware the apostles of charity! They are your enemies!

VOICE

Whom does he mean?

VOICE

He clearly means someone.

*[*ADAM *stands motionless in a shadow near the door]*

VOICE

What good is your talk, sir, when a man's bowels twist with hunger, and he has nothing to put on his back?

VOICE

Stupid! He had something else in mind.

VOICE

What?

[The din of the other voices drowns out theirs]

VOICE

But tell us, sir, why have you come here?

VOICE

Exactly.

STRANGER

I wanted to convince you that there are those who think of you, who fight for your rights. But they need your anger.

VOICE

Eh, sir! What's this about anger, and anger! Rebel, and you'll be put in jail, and that's that.

VOICE

Or they'll muzzle you. They have their ways.

STRANGER

That's the whole point: we must get the upper hand.

VOICE

But how?

STRANGER

Only give us your anger!

VOICE

There'll always be enough of that.

VOICE

What of it?

STRANGER

Because you take fright at the first hint of danger.

VOICE

Eh!

VOICE

It's easy for you to say that when you have enough food to sink your teeth into—

VOICE

And not a bad coat on your back.

VOICE

Yeah, yeah!

VOICE

But try to be one of us!

VOICE

Precisely!

VOICE

See how it is when your teeth chatter!

VOICE

Your teeth, yes—

VOICE

And try to deceive your stomach for a few days!

VOICE

Days . . . Exactly. Deceive your stomach!

VOICE *[Very loud]*

And then your jaw will drop, that's what!

*[*ADAM *stands aside. His words are scarcely audible in the dark]*

ADAM

Be one of us! Be one of us!

*[*ADAM *shakes his head. His body is trembling. The* STRANGER *tries to control the situation]*

STRANGER

You don't understand a word of what I've been saying. I am telling you that there are those who think of you. I've come only to make you aware of the strength you have in you.

[Someone in the crowd laughs]

VOICE

What strength, indeed?

[General laughter. Someone else speaks with great conviction]

VOICE

Suppose what you've been talking about happens. It wouldn't be bad. But you're talking and nothing comes of your words . . . That's the whole point . . .

VOICE

That's the point . . .

STRANGER

I have come to prepare you for the day something will happen. It will come. And it won't be long now.

VOICE

Let it come!

VOICE

But how do you know about it?

VOICE

Yes. How do you know?

*[*VOICES *are now louder here and there]*

VOICE

There've been others here, you know.

VOICE

There was one—remember?—who swore that everything was just around the corner. He talked and talked. Then what? He went away, and we're still here. And we're the same as before. End of story.

VOICE

And you, what do you intend to do? You'll remain the same as before, won't you?

STRANGER

But you must understand that we're talking about great masses. You're not alone. There are millions.

VOICE

You'll go away, and we shall remain.

STRANGER

You haven't understood anything—not one word.

VOICE

You're far away from us, and we're far away from you.

VOICE

You see, we're dumb. We know only one thing: only someone who lives among us knows all about us. Others don't know anything.

[They all begin to move away from him and return to their straw-covered bunks. Slowly they lie down. But some last comments are still heard on the event in which they have just participated]

VOICE

He's gone.

VOICE

One more benefactor.

VOICE

They all want to use us.

VOICE

But . . .

[The STRANGER *is left alone. He has not even noticed how he has stepped back a few yards so that now he finds himself nearer to the door and to* ADAM, *who still stands motionless in the darkness. The* STRANGER *whispers through clenched teeth]*

STRANGER

This is what I fear. They are the dregs of revolution.

*[*ADAM *suddenly answers him from the place where he is standing]*

ADAM

Yes, yes. There are people who are not yet ripe for the revolution that you . . .

*[*ADAM *breaks off in mid sentence. The poor, on their straw bunks, still share their thoughts in broken-off words, unfinished sentences]*

VOICE

Talk he did, but bring us something, no.

VOICE

What more do you want?

VOICE

You had some bright words—

VOICE

Put up fences—

ADAM

. . . revolution that you have in mind.

STRANGER

Not many.

ADAM

I think most of them. The great majority. Almost everybody.

STRANGER

No, you are mistaken. You would have to see the workers. These people are just louts. Life costs them nothing, so they shirk the struggle. Their anger does not hold out in the long run and is not much good for anything.

ADAM

In any event, there are still many people whom one must lift up.

STRANGER

Oh yes, that's what you want: life in an aura of beggary.

ADAM *[With an unexpected force of conviction]*

Yes, I am ready. I am ready. I think there are few who could lift themselves by the force of their anger.

. . . By the force of their own anger—well . . . feeling of bitterness, of wrong—you know?

. . . But they should lift themselves. Really lift themselves up.

STRANGER

What do you mean by that?

[All is quiet now in the bunks of the poor. The lamp dimly sheds light on those sleeping or falling asleep. Strangely, although ADAM *and his unknown companion are standing quite far from its circle of light, the outlines of their figures seem to profit more from its weak rays. It may be an instance of synesthesia so that the resonance of their voices seems to become visible. That must be why* ADAM *and the* STRANGER, *though standing further from the source of light, take a greater portion of it. It is still a poor, dim light, however.*

ADAM *remains silent and thoughtful for a while, as if he were looking for the words to answer, and the* STRANGER *feels obliged to repeat the question]*

What do you mean by that?

*[*ADAM *remains silent yet awhile, then replies with an effort, very slowly]*

ADAM

That I am very grateful to you.

STRANGER

What for?

ADAM

For a revelation.

STRANGER

Revelation?

ADAM

Yes . . . Of course, it is not the same for both of us. At a certain point it splits and goes off in different directions. Nonetheless, somewhere it is joined.

STRANGER

Why does it split?

ADAM

Because two different ways lead from the same point.

STRANGER

I know my way. Yours doesn't count. It is not the way of anger. And what matters here is anger alone. Great, universal anger. Human anger.

ADAM

Really? Did what happened here a short while ago not teach you anything? What happened was symbolic. There is a mass that wants to have, that simply wants to take! What will you do if it wants to have? Let us count on that force of anger. Let us assume that by the force of their anger that mass lifts itself up to take possession of many goods.

STRANGER

Of all goods!

ADAM

No, not all. That is impossible. Man's poverty is deeper than the resources of all goods.

STRANGER

That assertion is mad.

ADAM

Maybe. Nevertheless, it is true. Man's poverty is deeper than the resources of all those goods you are talking about. All those goods man can aspire to by the force of his anger.

STRANGER

I suspect I know what you mean and . . . I don't believe you.

ADAM

That is the point. You see, that is exactly the point. But I believe and I know. Oh my good sir, one man should not remain poor and another rich.

STRANGER

According to you it must be so.

ADAM

Not true. But I am sure, I believe, and I know that man is to aspire to all goods. To all. To the greatest of them too. But here anger fails; here Charity is essential.

STRANGER

You have no idea how great your responsibility is becoming for the wasted force of anger—wasted in all consciousness.

ADAM

Consciously I want only to rouse this anger in the right way. It is one thing to cultivate a just anger, make it ripen and reveal itself as a creative power, and another to exploit that anger, use it as raw material and abuse it.

STRANGER

Yes, yes, you will cultivate that anger only to stifle all its power again. But this time you will not succeed. It is too strong for that.

ADAM

Ah, have you never tried to feel the whole vastness of the values to which man is called? And do these stooping and hungry masses appeal to you only in the force of their anger? One must regard not one section of the truth but the whole truth.

STRANGER

You have the least right to talk to me like that.

[He is clearly embittered, though he speaks with a slight tinge of forbearance]

You are a typical artist. There is a strange contradiction between what you say and what you think.

ADAM

And yet I am not lying. You will admit that much.

STRANGER

Indeed . . . yes, it is very strange. You bypass both the lie and the truth. You are a true artist.

ADAM

Perhaps. Many people have said so.

STRANGER

And?

ADAM

Nothing. I am grateful to you. You have helped me free myself from the burden of those assertions.

STRANGER

How is that? You did not follow me.

ADAM

Indeed not. *[He points to the sleeping poor]* They did not follow you either.

STRANGER

They? . . . No, but they are not guilty to the same degree that you are. It is not their fault that they did not believe at once. Besides . . . revolution will absorb them. You are different because you have total awareness.

ADAM

Oh no . . . though I have more awareness than you.

STRANGER

Maybe.

ADAM

Yet they did not follow you.

STRANGER

Do you think that they will follow you? You think, no doubt, that you will be able to twist them around your little finger?

ADAM

No. I will follow them.

STRANGER

Stop wasting time on empty words.

ADAM

Oh no. There's an important difference.

STRANGER

All right. Have it your own way . . . But it's high time . . . Are you coming?

ADAM

No, I would like to stay.

STRANGER

Where will you sleep in this hovel?

ADAM

Well, they regard me almost as one of them now. I'll stay.

STRANGER

If you like. It will even be in your style.

ADAM

Exactly. I've managed to work out that style at last. It wasn't easy. But, well . . . I think it will be my style now . . .

[He reflects for a while]

No, it is not mine. I am indebted for it.

*[*ADAM *remains alone]*

III. The Brother's Day

[Let us now place a long span of years between what is to follow and those days, which accumulated in their inscrutable way. The whole deep-seated matter of becoming remains hidden in them beyond the shape of events. It has been revealed to us by certain tensions, as it were folds of the very matter of life, which thanks to them became tangible and capable of re-creation. Once these tensions had settled into permanent existence, the deep-seated matter emerged as the everyday substance of a transformed life. And their existence lasted for many years. Over the years the old tensions relaxed; becoming less pronounced, they subsided into the folds of life. None of them were lost or destroyed, but they became less acute. Thus they fell below the edge of drama, of becoming, but settled down as the pulse of life, beating regularly in the course of every day.

In the midst of those days, however, one came on which all the tensions resounded with a peculiar echo. The day itself brought no new drama, nor did it bring new tensions, but it strangely re-created the shape and substance of the former tensions. That is why there was something dramatic about it. Nonetheless the day did not resolve the drama or crush the hero in the classical manner with some superhuman disaster, burying in its ruins his love and thought. Oh no, his love and thought had long before been secured against destruction, for by their very nature they evade absolute catastrophe, though carrying the burden of many disasters, healing their traces from within. Just the same, the day was significant; it will not so much close our drama as, like an echo of old struggles, sketch once more its deep-seated shape, smoothed by the course of events.

It was one day in ADAM'S *life, one of so many days—and one of the last.*

The old poorhouse had long ago been changed to a shelter. Someone entering it today sees the same long, spacious room. Behind the wooden pillars supporting the ceiling—those are new—are rows of plank beds to right and left, as in the old days, but now more orderly. They are wooden, very poor and simple, but tidy. In the middle stands a long table, and in the background is a large crucifix made of dark wood.

Just now all the shadow is concentrated and calmly spread on the left. On the right a couple of brethren in worn gray habits are tidying up, talking to one another.]

ANTHONY

Has the Brother Superior come back?

SEBASTIAN

No. I last saw him this morning. He was driving his cart to the city.

ANTHONY

So he must be coming back soon. Those expeditions usually end by about eleven. *[After a while, he adds]* What do you think, Sebastian—how long can we go on like this?

SEBASTIAN

How's that? What do you mean?

ANTHONY

Well, begging is all right for a while, but one can have enough of it in the end.

SEBASTIAN

It's not our business. You have taken a vow.

ANTHONY

Many people have.

SEBASTIAN

No, Brother . . . these thoughts of yours are not good. Be watchful. I will pray for you.

ANTHONY

But listen. After all, everyone is entitled to use his brains . . . This cannot last.

SEBASTIAN

I suppose . . . our brains must be silent, since it does last.

ANTHONY

More and more people crowd in on us— people with their bellies swollen with hunger, foundlings, tramps, addicts. And all the people he finds in the streets or who come from goodness knows where think they have the right to be here.

And then, he drags drunken scoundrels out of the gutters and hauls them here on his old back.

SEBASTIAN

So what are you driving at, Anthony? This is what we took our vows for. And it's not our business. He thinks for us.

ANTHONY

We could make a couple of suggestions. After all, if we gave up all this begging, we could find the means to help more people. The cause would only profit by it.

SEBASTIAN

To Brother Superior poverty is dearer than anything.

ANTHONY

Precisely. But it doesn't seem right. Are we to help people, or to beg no matter what the results?

SEBASTIAN

I suppose you've had enough of begging?

ANTHONY

It's not that, but I simply don't understand why . . .

SEBASTIAN

I have taken vows, and so have you. Now carry the burden. After all, we didn't come here for our comfort. And then—we are indebted to him for everything. He made men of us.

[Other brethren come in carrying sacks]

That will do for today. Brother Superior won't let us get any more.

ANTHONY

And these methods, too . . .

SEBASTIAN

I'm telling you, Anthony, drive away these thoughts.

[A brother with a white apron wrapped around him comes in. It is BROTHER STEFAN, *the cook]*

STEFAN

You can start fetching water for the caldron, brethren.

A BROTHER

For the new one too?

STEFAN

Oh yes, yes. There is bound to be an even bigger crowd today.

A BROTHER

Let's go, John.

[The other brethren leave by the back door]

SEBASTIAN

How are you doing, Brother Stefan? We have more or less finished here.

STEFAN

I am not supposed to carry anything. You must know that I was once an awful sluggard. Our Brother Superior found me one day when I was begging—to get money for vodka, of course. He just said, "Come with me." I went. It was the strangest thing in my life. For I tell you I was an awful sluggard and a drunk—not that I had much money to spend on drink.

I wish today that I could change those days, go back and live them anew. Well, you can't get back the years. I am trying to make up for them, as much as I can.

ANTHONY

How do you make up for them, Brother Cook?

STEFAN

Well, it's not so difficult. One can please the Lord with anything. So Brother Superior teaches us. So I try to please the Lord by cooking the soup . . . But I have all this from him. Yes, yes.

And the strangest thing of all is that I followed him then.

SEBASTIAN

Oh yes, quite a few are indebted to him.

ANTHONY *[Like an echo]*

Quite a few . . .

[He goes out]

STEFAN

What's the matter with him?

SEBASTIAN

Oh, nothing. He seems to have been brooding a bit. He's going through a bad time. But it will pass.

STEFAN

Of course it will. We didn't come here to have an easy time. And there's enough to do penance for. It's just as well that someone has told us about that.

SEBASTIAN

Well, not everyone knows how to tell.

[A brother comes in]

BROTHER

Isn't Brother Superior supposed to be here soon?

SEBASTIAN

Oh yes. As soon as you hear the rumble of wheels on the stones and then the dull thud of his wooden crutch on the floor . . .

STEFAN

You have described it well, Sebastian. That's how it is, how it is repeated day after day at the same hour.

[The rumble of wheels is heard, then the thud of the crutch]

BRETHREN

Ah yes, here he is . . .

BROTHER SUPERIOR

[Crosses the threshold with an effort, lifting his wooden leg]

Has anyone been to see me, brethren?

STEFAN

No one has been here, Brother Superior.

BROTHER SUPERIOR

Unload the cart. There's enough in it for all our guests.

Well, what do you say to that? Isn't it beautiful? . . . You, Brother Stefan, are boiling water, not knowing what you will pour into it. And here a little cart drives in, just as the water boils. We only have to pour in what has been brought on the cart. In an hour everybody will sit down with a bowl. In two hours all the bowls will have been washed clean. Isn't that so? *[The brethren nod in silence]* Not only do we need no stores or larders, but our Father every day feeds us and clothes the poor . . .

SEBASTIAN

That's how it is, Brother Superior, that's how it is.

BROTHER SUPERIOR

And whom do you have to thank that you are not entangled, not surrounded by storerooms, pantries, coffers, moneybags, fears, thieves? . . . *[He laughs heartily while enumerating. The brethren share his joy]* Well? Whom? Whom?

STEFAN

You, I suppose, Brother.

BROTHER SUPERIOR

Not at all. Me, indeed. What an idea.

STEFAN

But it must be you.

BROTHER SUPERIOR

No, no! *[He seems to wait a while longer for the right answer. After a while]* The vows.

[The brethren agree and nod their heads]

SEBASTIAN

We were street beggars before.

BROTHER SUPERIOR

And now you are pledged to be beggars. That has changed everything. The vows have changed it all. You have come to love poverty, that's all.

STEFAN

And in the old days we hated it.

BROTHER SUPERIOR

But now you have come to love it and to be wed to it. So you see, there was no point in all those squabbles.

[All the brethren laugh heartily]

SEBASTIAN *[Suddenly stops laughing, speaks to himself]*

Some find it a burden, though . . .

[The general laughter is followed by a moment's pause. No one speaks. They think in silence. After a while BROTHER JANITOR *comes in and addresses the* BROTHER SUPERIOR*]*

BROTHER JANITOR

Brother Superior, a young man asks to talk to you.

BROTHER SUPERIOR

Let him in, Brother.

*[*BROTHER JANITOR *goes out. After a while the* YOUNG MAN *comes in]*

YOUNG MAN

I want to talk to you, Brother.

BROTHER SUPERIOR

I am at your service.

YOUNG MAN

I'll come straight to the point. The sort of life you lead appeals to me. Please admit me to your brotherhood, Brother Superior.

[The BROTHER SUPERIOR *remains silent]*

I have thought about it for a long time. This is the only way to save my failing faith. The point on which faith is swaying like a boat under the blows of the wind remains somewhere in the mind. It may be simply the pride of the mind . . .

Under the boat lies a bay. And the boat's anxiety reaches it. It is as if someone were splitting the bay apart from below.

BROTHER SUPERIOR

What do these words mean?

YOUNG MAN

How else can I describe the strange expansion in a man of something. . . intrinsic . . . human. But no . . . In any case, the course is stormy. Yes, as if someone were splitting the bay from the bottom.

BROTHER SUPERIOR

I am beginning to understand something of what you say. But what do you expect from us?

YOUNG MAN

Well, Brother, it is something like this: music is confirmed by the great inner silence of all unmusical receivers in our awareness while the volume of our sensitive centers is increased. The faith that is failing must be saved in a similar way. One must look for the relevant centers; those that are sensitive, pulsating with its strength.

BROTHER SUPERIOR

And has this brought you to us?

YOUNG MAN

Yes.

BROTHER SUPERIOR

What is your name?

YOUNG MAN

Hubert.

BROTHER SUPERIOR

Very well, Hubert. You may remain with us for a time. Then you will choose.

HUBERT

I have already chosen.

BROTHER SUPERIOR

That is not the end. You must remember that we do not choose; we are simply chosen . . .

HUBERT

Yes.

BROTHER SUPERIOR

And are you sure of that, too?

HUBERT

Well, that's the point. Can one be quite sure? One can only search, hope to find one's way . . .

BROTHER SUPERIOR

I think, Hubert, you must be very tired.

HUBERT

Oh yes.

BROTHER SUPERIOR

You must take a rest.

*[*HUBERT *remains silent]*

You have concerned yourself with music a great deal, isn't that so?

HUBERT

Yes, in the past. How do you know about it, Brother?

BROTHER SUPERIOR

It's not hard to guess. You think and judge things in musical terms.

HUBERT

Yes. I looked for a way through from that angle. In vain.

BROTHER SUPERIOR

No doubt. The approach is usually difficult.

HUBERT

You say so, Brother. Of course, Brother Superior knows these matters better than anyone. That's why I have come here . . .

BROTHER SUPERIOR

Well . . .

HUBERT

There must have been a moment in your life, Brother, when you faced the need to make similar decisions.

[A moment's silence. HUBERT *waits anxiously for the reply]*

BROTHER SUPERIOR *[Speaks very slowly, with obvious effort]*

One cannot infer anything from this apparent analogy.

HUBERT

You say apparent, Brother. Should you not rather say striking?

BROTHER SUPERIOR

No!

HUBERT

No?

BROTHER SUPERIOR

One must not judge by appearances. You remember how old Isaac made a mistake, choosing wrongly between Jacob and Esau. One must not judge by the coverings that surround human lives. What matters here is whether you have been chosen . . .

HUBERT

How can one be sure about that?

BROTHER SUPERIOR

First, one must have an altogether new view of the world. You do not have it. Now that makes a difference, my dear sir; that makes a difference. It is one thing to apply to the world the rules by which musical tonalities come together and disperse—that is immensely interesting, immensely beautiful and sublime—but it is quite another to see the scope of misery and degradation in the world and to know, to know precisely, how God views it all, what misery brings Him closer to men and what separates Him from them.

HUBERT

I think I would know how to judge.

BROTHER SUPERIOR

With what? With a disappointed musical vision? Do you know at least the greatest misery of man before God? *[A moment's silence]* That misery must not be looked for at the limits of man, at his peripheries, but in him, precisely at the point from which his highest uplift should begin.

HUBERT

Yes, I feel I know what you mean, Brother. The significance of opposites.

BROTHER SUPERIOR

We usually misjudge things . . .

Charity and wrong have in reality different meanings and begin somewhere other than where one usually assumes . . .

But to see that, one needs this kind of vision. Without it one will constantly commit blunders. You are searching for that vision, aren't you?

HUBERT

I think so, yes. It's strange: something that wrecks my life but at the same time integrates it.

BROTHER SUPERIOR

[Remains silent for a moment, then quite suddenly asks]

And what is going to happen to your art?

HUBERT

What do you think, Brother? . . .

BROTHER SUPERIOR

Because, you see, here we have a different sort of art. How can I explain it to you? . . . You see . . . the coefficients of raw material, talent, and effort are distributed differently here.

HUBERT

I don't know; I don't know anything. I am in the dark.

BROTHER SUPERIOR

That in itself need not be harmful.

HUBERT

Please help me.

BROTHER SUPERIOR

Poor boy, it seems to me that you are looking for solutions that are too bold. You must not try to change like this; you must let changes grow slowly. You need patience. I do not believe, of course, that you are really threatened with a loss of faith. Nonetheless, you are looking for strong stimuli—and not in the sphere of emotions but in the sphere of reality. That is very good.

HUBERT

Yes? Brother Superior wishes to reassure me.

BROTHER SUPERIOR

You see, your case is not easy. Many things have not yet matured. You are really still on the other side. But something is pulling you over.

HUBERT

You have defined it well, Brother.

BROTHER SUPERIOR

I know, I know. But I am still not sure.

HUBERT

Of what?

BROTHER SUPERIOR

Your vision.

HUBERT

What vision? You keep talking about a vision, Brother.

BROTHER SUPERIOR

Ah yes. It can happen that one gropes in the dark for a long time.

HUBERT

I have come here for light.

BROTHER SUPERIOR

Yes, yes. But I am afraid that you could go blind . . . The art we have here is different, quite different. So when you are deprived of the other and this one does not mature, it will be very dark. I don't know how long the darkness can last.

HUBERT

But what do you have in mind? You must be judging others by yourself.

[A pause in their dialogue. There is no reply for a while]

Brother Superior, if you do not help me, who will?

BROTHER SUPERIOR

But I want to help you.

HUBERT

Thank you.

BROTHER SUPERIOR

You must not imagine that this will mean: stay with us for good.

HUBERT

No? What does it mean then?

BROTHER SUPERIOR

It means rather: go on searching.

HUBERT

Why?

BROTHER SUPERIOR

I will not tell you. I cannot answer you fully, but it is so.

HUBERT

Go on searching. But for what? I think I have searched enough. I have searched among so many truths. After all, these things can mature only in this way. Philosophy . . . art . . . After all, truth finally does rise to the top, like oil on water. This is how life reveals it to us—slowly, partially, but constantly. Besides, the truth is in us, in every man; there it begins to cleave to life. We carry it in ourselves; it strengthens us in our weakness . . . And so it is in the first, the second, the hundredth man. What is truth? What is truth? Where is it?

Life consists of people in whom it flows broadly, uniting in its outlet with a new level of light in eyes that are wide open. Yes, yes . . . there are people simply united with truth, who do not leave its orbit but remain in its embrace, thanks to their inner equilibrium.

BROTHER SUPERIOR *[Silent for a while, at last replies]*
Well, precisely. You ought to go on searching for it still unaided. A man like you must not take shortcuts . . . or . . .

HUBERT
Or?

BROTHER SUPERIOR
Or make the way too easy.

HUBERT
So, Brother Superior, you refuse . . .

BROTHER SUPERIOR
I advise against it. How can I tell whether the same thing will mature in you that has matured in me? Up to now there has been only darkness. And groping in the dark.

HUBERT
But you condemn me to further misery.

BROTHER SUPERIOR
That does not matter. And it is necessary for you to become poor.

HUBERT
How is that? I have lost so much already . . .

BROTHER SUPERIOR
That does not prove anything yet. *[After a while]* And then . . . it is hard to think that two people should tread the same path so closely. Would this accord with His generosity? God is generous in His ways.

HUBERT
Is that the whole reason?

BROTHER SUPERIOR

I do not know. There is no reason really. But I know you ought to go away from here. You are called somewhere else.

HUBERT

Where?

BROTHER SUPERIOR

These things clarify themselves as the occasion arises. Sometimes in an hour.

[Pause. A moment's silence]

HUBERT

For some time now a certain thought has been forcing itself upon me. It is stubborn.

BROTHER SUPERIOR

Please tell me . . .

HUBERT

I have come to you, Brother Superior, convinced that no one else can solve my difficulties as well as you. After all, they reflect your own.

BROTHER SUPERIOR

That does not mean anything. But . . . what is it? . . .

HUBERT

[Concentrates with an effort, trying to find words for what he wants to utter. Then he says slowly]

Brother Superior, do you simply want to erase all your life in me?

*[*ALBERT, *the* BROTHER SUPERIOR, *lowers his head, gloomy for a moment. Then he looks up again and gives* HUBERT *a penetrating, though very calm, look]*

BROTHER SUPERIOR

God is too good. *[He shakes his head]* God is too generous. Too generous.

*[*HUBERT *does not lower his eyes. He does not seem to be quite convinced because he repeats emphatically, though in a very low voice]*

HUBERT

Would you simply wish, Brother Superior, to cross out in me what all your life has been? Impossible! Impossible!

[They take leave of each other without another word. ALBERT *is unmoved, almost as if nothing has happened to him. A brother approaches and whispers to him. He replies]*

BROTHER SUPERIOR

Ah well, well.

[The brother leaves. After a while BROTHER ANTHONY *enters]*

ANTHONY

I would like a word with you, Brother Superior.

BROTHER SUPERIOR

Maybe later we'll find a suitable moment.

ANTHONY

I'd rather talk now. It's a simple matter. I've had enough of this begging.

BROTHER SUPERIOR

You are not the first.

ANTHONY

I think you could do infinitely more good if you put an end to your obstinacy.

BROTHER SUPERIOR

But Brother, all the good here is done through poverty.

ANTHONY

Through beggary, through walking about with sacks for begging?

BROTHER SUPERIOR

And what do you think? Would any of your homeless, with their hunger-swollen bellies, believe us if they saw us carrying something different from what they carry on their own backs?

ANTHONY

Whether they believe or not, what does it matter? I was one of them, so I know. Today they simply make demands.

BROTHER SUPERIOR

Not at all. The most important thing is that they believe.

ANTHONY

And in your view they have time to think about belief. I was like them; I know. They don't think. If they did, they would have to stop making demands. It is enough to give.

BROTHER SUPERIOR

That's not true. One must rouse them from such thoughtlessness.

ANTHONY

What for?

BROTHER SUPERIOR

To teach them to demand even more. Have you still not grasped that, living among us? To demand even more. To search for more.

And you are wrong at that. They do think about it. If they think about anything at all, they think about that one thing.

O Anthony, Anthony. Have you not understood this yet?

ANTHONY

No, I never could understand it. I could never understand what you had in mind, Albert. And I do not think I have been the only one.

BROTHER SUPERIOR

But I never made a secret of it. I wanted you to know it—all of you.

ANTHONY

Yet what can you do if someone has not understood you? I'm not the only one. There are more like me, though only I have the courage to tell you about it, Brother Superior.

BROTHER SUPERIOR

Thank you for doing so, Anthony.

ANTHONY

They do not understand you, either, though they agree with you. That's the easy way. They live at your expense. They depend on your thinking. They do not think for themselves. That's why I ask you again, Brother Superior: what do you teach us? Why do you make us live from hand to mouth and beg? I am asking you this in front of them all.

[During their conversation the room has in fact begun to fill up with brethren. Mealtime approaches, so the benches gradually fill. The brethren stand in their places, silent. This silence makes the scene unusual, for it looks simply like a silent judgment of ALBERT. BROTHER SUPERIOR *takes in the situation. Is he suddenly facing a void where he had intended to bequeath all his riches? Maybe he has been wrong all the time about them—the people he thought he was converting. Now they unwittingly judge him.* ALBERT *knows that in* ANTHONY'S *words they all accuse him, so* ALBERT *glances at those assembled, looking for a verdict in their faces. When he does not find it, he begins to speak softly]*

BROTHER SUPERIOR

My brethren, I have taken everything from you; I have demanded everything of you. I did not deceive you with any promises. Did I have the right to do this?

I have also imposed a burden on you. But I looked deep in every one of you for its support, where hatred of the cursed burden was to transform itself into the love of it . . .

[He stops speaking, remains silent for a while]

You know by now that I am talking about the cross, about our common cross, which transforms a man's fall into good and his slavery into freedom.

[From the group of gray brothers, silently attentive as if lifeless, one figure detaches itself. An old man takes a few steps in ALBERT'S *direction, then makes a movement with his hand, as if to stroke* ALBERT'S *shoulder]*

OLD MAN

Brother, Brother Superior, Albert—

[These words creak in the void like the arm of a crane. ALBERT *senses their presence but supports himself on them very cautiously, as if testing their strength]*

BROTHER SUPERIOR

Did I have the right to do it? After all, even your poverty was your own . . .

[At this moment ALBERT *feels the surge of an unknown force. His eyes shine strangely. He says]*

It was a game in which I knew I was not alone. In each of you I knew about poverty and about Him. They remained apart for a long time. With all my strength I tried to bring them closer together. In the past there you were—paupers—with the wind of desolation blowing over your misery. Ever since you have come closer to Him, your fall has changed into the cross, and your slavery into freedom.

*[*BROTHER SEBASTIAN *raises his hands as high as possible, to his temples. He does not follow* ALBERT *but, in the center of the room, speaks through his tears]*

BROTHER SEBASTIAN

Slavery into freedom . . . fall into the cross . . . Oh yes, Albert, oh yes . . .

BROTHER SUPERIOR

The Son of God is all freedom. Without a trace of slavery.

ANTHONY *[Who has been standing, silent]*

But what of it? What of it, even if He is all freedom? He was once.

BROTHER SUPERIOR

He still is.

ANTHONY

He is. I believe. You told us to believe in Him, pray to Him, imitate Him. Very well. You said, "Be poor, because He did not have a place where He could rest His head." Very well. We listened to you willingly because you did that. There was no deception in you. And yet . . .

*[*ANTHONY *cannot find the right words. The silence becomes heavy. After a while* ALBERT *repeats his last sentence. He speaks it quietly but firmly, almost obstinately]*

BROTHER SUPERIOR

He still is. He constantly reaches souls and in them re-creates . . . Himself!

*[*ALBERT'S *last word resonates strangely. He is lost in thought again]*

Clearly he did not reach deep enough . . . Clearly . . .

[Whom he refers to is not clear. Suddenly ALBERT *turns around and takes a few steps toward the crucifix, darkly visible at the back of the room. All heads turn in that direction.* BROTHER SUPERIOR *does not rest his forehead against the cross. He stands still.* ANTHONY *follows him, as if in a trance.* ALBERT *speaks]*

Someone is to blame. There were three of us.

[He lifts his eyes to the crucifix]

He—no.

[Slowly he half turns toward ANTHONY. *This movement seems to require an effort]*

You—no.

[A momentary silence]

Maybe—I . . . *[He is lost in thought. But then he briskly approaches the benches]* The bell has rung for the Angelus.

[The brethren begin to pray. Some places remain empty. ANTHONY *is dazed. He seems to struggle with himself for a while. Then he returns to his seat and covers his face with his hands. A clatter of feet is heard in the hall, then some quieter sounds, as of tools—spades and pickaxes—being put away. The door opens and a few brethren slip into the room. Without uttering a word they walk to their seats and begin to pray. All the benches are occupied. When the newly arrived brethren have finished their prayer, they sit down. The* BROTHER SUPERIOR *turns to the new arrivals]*

Well, how is it with you?

FIRST BROTHER

We were let off early from work.

BROTHER SUPERIOR

Why was that?

FIRST BROTHER

Something's happening in the city.

SECOND BROTHER

There are no trams or cars.

FIRST BROTHER

They say the electricity and gas have been turned off. The workers have laid down their tools. They are marching in many places, chanting slogans.

BROTHER SUPERIOR

Even this morning I noticed an unusual excitement.

Yes, yes . . . Such a sudden outbreak, though . . . Explosives must have been ready. Only a spark was needed . . .

[Another brother appears in the doorway]

And where do you come from, Brother?

BROTHER COLLECTOR

From my collecting rounds. They are closing restaurants and shops all over the city. The police are everywhere.

BROTHER SUPERIOR

Well, come and sit with us, Brother.

[Suddenly, at the end of the table one of the brethren gets up. It is ANTHONY*]*

ANTHONY

You see, a lot of good your begging will do you now!

BROTHER SUPERIOR *[Turns smiling toward him]*

Indeed, Brother Anthony?

ANTHONY

Didn't I say so? Didn't I? . . .

[Becomes disconcerted by BROTHER SUPERIOR'S *smile]*

BROTHER SUPERIOR

[Becomes thoughtful, then speaks very slowly, as if weighing every word]

I have known about this for a long time. It had to come.

BROTHER COLLECTOR

You knew, Brother Superior? What did you know?

BROTHER SUPERIOR

[Looks in his direction penetratingly, but as if through a haze]

About anger. About great, just anger.

BROTHER COLLECTOR

And?

BROTHER SUPERIOR

Ah well. You know that anger has to erupt, especially if it is great.

[He stops]

And it will last, because it is just.

[He becomes even more deeply lost in thought. Then he adds one sentence, as if to himself, though everyone listens attentively]

I know for certain, though, that I have chosen a greater freedom.

[This was one of the last days in the life of BROTHER SUPERIOR*]*

RADIATION OF FATHERHOOD

A Mystery

by Fr. Karol Wojtyła (Pope John Paul II), 1964

translated by Bolesław Taborski

For there are three that bear record
in heaven, the Father, the Word, and
the Holy Ghost: and these three are one.
And there are three that bear witness
in earth, the Spirit, and the water,
and the blood: and these three agree in one.
1 JOHN 5

Speakers[1]

ADAM

CHORUS

WOMAN, also called the MOTHER

MONICA, a child

[1] List prepared by the editor

Part I. Adam

1. "I" And Metamorphoses

ADAM

For many years I have lived like a man exiled from my deeper personality yet condemned to probe it. During those years I have toiled unceasingly to reach it but have often thought with horror that it was disappearing, blurred among the processes of history, in which what matters is numbers, mass. All this is connected with the name Adam given to me. Through this name I must encounter every man; at the same time everything in this name that every man contributes can be made commonplace or even be devalued. I have a difficult name. How often have I thought that my footsteps should be wiped out, that I had to obliterate myself, so that I could identify with every man whose history is written by the crowd. Is it written only from without?

The thought constantly returns that I ought to find myself in every man—searching not from without but from within.

[Many people enter. Haphazardly and chaotically, they fill the space around ADAM. *He does not turn to them immediately but feels their presence]*

Here are the people who emerge from the gates of the steelworks... They wear workers' overalls and leather jackets.

Here are the passersby: they overtake me at the street corner without looking in my direction.

Here are those who find their way home and quietly shut the door behind them or slam their garden gate.

Some look back intently; others do not even turn their eyes.

All of them pass by.

Everyone carries in himself an unrealized substance called humanity.

This is connected with the painful experience of so many generations. Can one hide in it? Or on the contrary, should it be brought out of hiding, like an object one admires or despises? O humanity, which can be filled to its upper limit or weakened to its lowest! What distance separates those limits?

"I" and the metamorphoses of so many people. I face this always.

I decided to place one man apart and make him a common denominator for all men, letting him be present in all yet not be any of them. Then I had a good look at that man and recognized him: it was myself.

They all pass by.

I look toward those who have gone away, having fallen in the battle. It is true that we all fight—but are we all soldiers?

I look toward those who approach. Is it true that through my fault "approach" means the same as "draw near to death?"

2. The Analysis of Loneliness

ADAM

I find it difficult to think about this.

Although I am like the man who can be placed apart and made a common denominator for all men, I am still lonely. It is easier for me to feel lonely than to think about death. Nobody calls loneliness a sin, and I find it easier to feel lonely than guilty of sin. But I know who Adam was and who he is. He stopped once on the frontier between fatherhood and loneliness. Who cut him off from men; who made him lonely in the midst of them all? What if he became lonely of his own free will? What if he became lonely in order to graft that loneliness onto others? Can he say today, It is easier for me to feel lonely than guilty? After all, he made himself lonely in the midst of them all because he made them lonely.

"Ah," he said then about himself, "I could not bear fatherhood; I could not be equal to it. I felt totally helpless—and what had been a gift became a burden to me. I threw off fatherhood like a burden. For that matter, was I to be a father, or would people merely associate me always with the idea of the Father?"

He is lonely, I thought. What will make me more like Him, that is to say, independent of everything? Ah, to stand apart from everything, so that I could be only within myself! I should then be closest to You. I later said to Him, complaining, "You could have left me in the sphere of fertility (I would somehow have reconciled myself to nature) without placing me in the depths of a fatherhood to which I am unequal! Why did You plant it in the soil of my soul? Was it not enough that You had it in Yourself?

"Well, what if people had multiplied out of me, what if they had peopled the earth? You could have left me apart from them. There would have been an 'outward Adam' to flourish and grow and an 'inward Adam,' a lonely one. Why ask that he allow the radiation of Your Fatherhood to enter him so that he can refract it as a prism refracts light?"

If having formed me of clay, You had said: Clay, go on forming, I would have formed many a thing. You know best the staggering temperatures of kilns where clay is baked—You for whom the entire computation of atoms is the simplest intuition, not a compilation of figures and formulas. I would surely pluck out many more things from Your intelligence and implant them in my world—calling, It is I, it is I, that is true—but that world would be Yours anyway. For what am I?. . . I who am transient all the time. With every step—not with every generation now but with every step—my life is breaking off . . . and constantly begins anew.

Did You have to touch my thought with Your knowledge that means giving birth? Did You have to touch my will with the love that is fulfillment? I cannot give birth in this way! In me love never fulfills itself. That is why You were disappointed in me. Did I not call from the start, "Leave me my loneliness"? I know I called in spite of myself. But even more in spite of You.

I will say more: I have decided to throw the word "mine" out of my vocabulary. How can I use it when I know that everything is Yours? Although You yourself do not give birth with every human birth, still he who does give birth is Yours. And I myself am more Yours than mine. I have learned that I must not call what is Yours mine, must not say, think, feel it to be mine. I must free, divest myself of it; I must not have or want anything of my own ("mine" means "own").

Is it really so?

I am afraid of the word "mine," though at the same time I cherish its meaning. I am afraid because this word always puts me face to face with You. An analysis of the word "mine" always leads me to You. And I would rather give up using it than find its ultimate sense in You. For I want to have everything through myself, not through You. To want this is nonsense, but haven't many other people harnessed themselves to serve it?

Thus the thought never leaves me that You have been disappointed in me. When I give birth, I do it to become lonely among those born, because I pass on to them the germ of loneliness. In the midst of a multitude, are they not more and more lonely? Numbers do not engender love, and loneliness rather engenders strife than makes one independent. Just think, I have not known, even for a moment, the fulfillment that is in You!

Can I ask, after all this, that You forgive me for executing my plan with such obstinacy? For continually evading Your Fatherhood and gravitating toward my loneliness, so that You must reveal Yourself as if in an external vacuum? But I am only a common denominator of all men, or a common word that can be put outside the brackets.

[Again in ADAM'S *space the same people appear who were there before, but they come nearer, as if they wanted to surround him]*

Leave me! Do not always find your way to me! I am only the common denominator of you all—do not try to find anything else in me!

An association with the idea of the Father—between the upper borderline of man filled with humanity and the lower one of humanity destroyed in man, this always remains: association with the idea of the Father . . . association with the idea of the Father.

[The people surrounding ADAM *step back a little but do not leave]*

3. The Threshold Crossed by Woman

ADAM

Because You execute Your plan. You are determined and Your plans are irreversible. The strangest thing always transpires in the end: that You are never against me. You enter into what I call loneliness, and You overcome my resistance. Can one say that You force Your way in or only that You enter through a door that is open anyway? You did not make me closed; You did not quite close me. Loneliness is not at the bottom of my being at all; it grows at a certain point. The fissure through which You enter is far deeper. You enter—and slowly begin to shape me. You shape and develop me in spite of what I imagine about my ego and about other people, yet You do it in harmony with what I am. This I cannot deny. Yet can I wonder that You are stronger in me than myself? You want me to love. You aim at me through a child, through a tiny daughter or son—and my resistance weakens. Nothing remains of the loneliness with which I resist You. You, however, express Yourself deeply. Gradually I cease to feel that You express Yourself in me, and I begin to think that I express myself in myself. And it is always so until love gives pain, the pain caused by lack of fulfillment, a lack of my ego in the beloved or of the beloved's in me . . . But precisely at that moment one sees most clearly that man cannot reject from his consciousness the word "mine." This word follows him all the time, and he goes where it leads him. And this word cancels loneliness.

The Woman has entered loneliness. She has entered and enters all the time. I see her following in the path of all people, who keep asking for me. I, however, direct their attention to her and ask if they know her. They grow silent then and begin to look toward her. In her, new life has been conceived. So she walks with extreme caution. Even from outside she tries to enfold *the Being she carries in her womb. She is a Mother.*

[Everything ADAM *describes happens as he speaks. The people scattered in groups in* ADAM'S *space turn their eyes toward the* WOMAN, *and when she has passed by and disappeared from view, they begin to move in the same direction. After a while, all are turned away from* ADAM. *They look toward her]*

4. Between Meeting and Fulfillment

ADAM

After a long time I came to understand that you do not want me to be a father unless I become a child. That is why Your Son came into the world. He is entirely Yours. In Him the word "mine" finds complete justification; it can be spoken credibly by Him. Without such a justification and credibility this word is a risk—love is a risk, too. Why did you inflict on me the love that in me must be a risk? And now Your Son takes on Himself all the risk of love.

How much the word "mine" must hurt when it turns out later to mean "not mine." I think with awe about the strain and toil of Your Son, about the magnitude of His love. How much did He take on Himself? What voids did He fill? How great is the void He must fill! After all, in all of us the common denominator of our loneliness remains, and in it, against all the logic of existence, "mine" still tries to force out "Yours." Could I too become a son? I did not want to be one. I did not want to accept the suffering caused by risking love. I thought I would not be equal to it. My eyes were too fixed on myself, and in such a situation love is most difficult.

When Your Son came, I remained the common denominator of man's inner loneliness. Your Son wants to enter it. He wants to because He loves. Loneliness opposes love. On the borderline of loneliness, love must become suffering: Your Son has suffered.

And now there are two of us in the history of every man: I who conceive and bear loneliness and He in whom loneliness disappears and children are born anew.

Many people look on Your Son's life, on His suffering and death; many have gone the way He takes. I do not stand apart from Him; I do not oppose Him. I admire and worship Him, but at the same time I resist Him. I do it to some extent because I cannot afford to do anything else. Sometimes this is connected with a mirage of greatness. But I find it even harder to retain a sense of my own greatness than a sense of my loneliness. In loneliness one can hide and forget. But what am I to do when I keep falling off pedestals? What am I to do when people tormented by other people, crucified like Your Son, return and ask the same questions: Where has the exiled father gone to? Where has the punishing father come from?

*[*ADAM'S *space suddenly fills again with people. They are the same people who had earlier moved away in the direction taken by the* WOMAN, *looking toward her. The horizon has darkened, and these people, near* ADAM *again, circle around him and repeat in a chorus the questions he has just asked]*

CHORUS

Where has the exiled father gone to?
Where has the punishing father come from?

ADAM

Two thoughts just came to me. The first thought: Fathers will not return to themselves, so you are not wanted; go, mix with the crowd now, and lose yourself in it. The second thought: Fathers return through their children; the father always revives in the soil of a child's soul.

5. Mother

ADAM

That second thought brought liberation with it. The hands stretched out ready to snatch and maybe tear me to pieces—or what is worse, to merge me with the crowd—turned back. Soon I heard a voice. I heard it before I was able to see who spoke. It was the Woman, the Mother.

MOTHER

Do not be afraid. This must hurt. It is a pain like the pain of birth. A woman knows infinitely more about giving birth than a man. She knows it particularly through the suffering that accompanies childbearing. Still, motherhood is an expression of fatherhood. It must always go back to the father to take from him all that it expresses. In this consists the radiation of fatherhood.

One returns to the father through the child. And the child, in turn, restores to us the bridegroom in the father. This is very simple and ordinary. The whole world is full of it. One must enter the radiation of fatherhood, since only there does everything become fully real. For at no point can the world be fiction, the inner world even less than the external world. Just think! Think, all of you: one must choose to give birth! You have not thought about this. One must choose to give birth even more than to create.

In this consists the radiation of fatherhood. It is no metaphor, but reality. The world cannot depend on metaphor alone, the inner world even less than the external world.

We return to the father through the child. And the child in turn restores to us the bridegroom in the father. Do not separate love. Love is a unity.

[The people assembled in ADAM'S *space listen with growing attention. The* WOMAN *is talking more and more to them and for them. They are encompassed by a common light—not full light, perhaps, but low light.* ADAM, *however, remains outside its circle. He talks very slowly]*

ADAM

It still seems to me that somehow I evade the substance in which I am embedded. Man is not only born but also dies, not only gives life but also inflicts death. To be able to choose, one must first know all. Can I say that I know all? No, I cannot say that . . .

[He is silent for a while]

I have found, though, that I am not "lonely." I am, much more, "closed."

[The CHORUS *is silent]*

Part II. The Experience of a Child

[The external situation drawn here is, step by step, an outcome, or offshoot, of the inner situation. This is most important. The scenery is at times intimate: a solitary room, whose most significant piece of furniture is a big armchair. There is also a writing desk and a bookshelf; a flower vase on each of them. Later the scenery changes (for this purpose it may be necessary only to remove the furniture), and we have the edge of a forest. For all the action in this part has something of wandering or striving about it: the inner striving finds its counterpart in the external action. Only two persons take part: ADAM, *who becomes a father, and a child, whom we will call* MONICA.*]*

1. The Album

ADAM

Let us sit here in the armchair, under this lamp with its shade, and take the album into our hands. Here are snapshots from the earliest years. A young woman is holding a baby in her arms. Its oval face is different now, but the eyes have the same glee. The history of those eyes: through all these pictures they remain, more than anything; they unite everything in one stream, which absorbs more and more traits; in them rests the identity of the soul.

Oh, look! If only I could put this picture into a projector—
here is a girl of two with a huge dog.
The dog was called Arpad; he had a sweet mouth
when he approached the little girl, wagging his wispy tail
and kindly holding out his paw . . . You innocent little creature,
how obedient all nature is to you; even this giant does not
  bark—
the first picture.

Now the goat: the projector shows huge horns and a slanting
  head.
You're struggling, little one? Not afraid of the horns? The tiny

hands beat with a stick
as if the horns were the keys of an instrument hidden in the goat,
on which, little one, you want to play something, something that is also in you now—
the second picture.

The third picture: hens—big hens and little chicks,
among whom you dream away each day in the yard, picking flowers
as they peck at their seed. Then you come in through the French windows,
and they, returning to the roost, pass the night in the henhouse,
while you sleep in a little bed beyond the French windows,
past the verandah, beyond the hall, beyond the kitchen and beyond grandpa's room.
You sleep with mommy. Daddy is far away . . .

There is no daddy in this album, nor will he ever appear there.
But is he not like the hidden sun that warms your little body,
oh, here in the fourth picture?

The fourth picture:
you are sitting under a parasol, hiding from the hot sun.
Though the sun cannot be seen in the snapshot, we feel it all around and in you too.
There are many snapshots in this album—a whole roll of film—
all clipped together in one book and in the book one story:
but the eyes are the same—the soul's identity.

(The album ends at this point—but I remember what follows.)

When she was still at primary school—I remember her laughter,
the free, girlish laughter—she was called squeaker,
little squeaker. This name was meant to describe her laughter,
which sometimes changed to a squeak—the squeak of a shy nestling.
When she was still a little girl, she was more outside me,
though it appeared to be the other way around . . .
She did her homework in the afternoon, quick at algebra

though she blotched her Polish exercise book, often crossing out words.
Then geography and later still a drawing lesson—
and at last freedom, freedom: one can run along the long corridor
without upsetting things; one can spin around
without even touching anything; one can squeak. . .
"Daddy has come." She creeps up furtively in her soft slippers,
then suddenly tugs at his sleeve and nestles close to him: "Here I am."
Poor child, I thought, poor child, *she will never see her father* . . .
"Do you know, I have a daddy now," she once confided to her mother.
"Do you know, I have a daddy now . . ."

2. The Child's Sanctuary

MONICA

1
My father's history in me. The beginning is lost in the darkness
of my soul, a child's, long before the wandering begins
to trace his presence, because first there was absence.
When I was a little girl, I ran briskly on the grass,
I drove hens from the yard, I slept in my little bed with my teddy bear,
then when I had had enough of the teddy bear, I slept with a doll.
In the spring I picked flowers for someone, for someone, for someone . . .
Daddy was not by me; Daddy was not on earth.
I want my daddy on earth, close, very close to my heart.
I must find him, pluck him out of the still picture,
and from all my hope give birth, give birth, give birth . . .
Many a time I took flowers, and when he was not in the room,
I put them on his desk and left immediately.
He would recognize my presence

from the flowers in the vase near his books.
He would think I am in her heart and look for me in his own heart,
if only for a while.
When I was far away, I would pluck a flower while writing a letter
and put the flower in the envelope together with a sheet of my clumsy writing,
for I do not find writing easy and cannot express
what is in me.
But he would know everything from the flower
that the postman brought him with my letter and my thoughts
and, above all, my heart.

Would you believe it? . . .
If you were not on earth, I would look with pity
on the album of my infant days—that other one would not know this one;
this one would not know her. Everything would be split,
disunified—and yet it does.

2

My father's history in me begins with his absence,
yet he must have been there all the time, though I did not feel him at all.
Perfectly unified with mother, I did not know that he would one day break loose,
for he is embedded in me with his roots, *like another, parallel, tree trunk.*
I have just realized: the double trunk among so many trees
in the forest. What a wealth of boughs and branches and, high up, leaves;
everything grows out of one system, out of common roots.
So did father grow in me through mother,
and I was their unity,
that segment of the mass of the tree through which both trunks grow.

It seemed strange to me that I was the thickest segment
(for further on the tree divides into two parallel trunks,
and each of them is thinner).
And so I looked astonished
at the thoughts that passed into me from the divided tree.
So father grew in me through mother—but for a long time I did not perceive him,
did not feel his absence because his roots were embedded in me.

3

How I do love you, my father,
my strange father, born in my soul,
Father, you who were born in me to give birth to me.
I did not know for many years that you had grown so much in me;
for so long I did not know your face, your warm eyes, the bend of your profile—
until the day I linked the immense longing in my soul
precisely with you,
until the day the absence had to become the presence
it had once been.
My father, I am fighting for you. Be in me, as I want to be in you.

4

Now we are in the forest. The trees climb high.
The last little triangle of light disappears from a sheltered creek
between the isle of branches and the trembling waves of air.
The forest evening, small forest evening, rises to a large evening
that will soon fill the horizon.
When will be spoken what is contained in you and me,
what lies in the depth of consciousness and must wait for words?
Being together, shall we find one day the moments for such words
that bring to the surface what really is deep down;

shall we confirm for every day the existence of what is?
I discover this world in you slowly and all at once:
it is the world of my father—how much I want to be in it!

[She hums]

(A small dark street among trees—and there are many such streets,
running in many directions. Which ones will meet?
I don't know anymore if you're sitting in a deep armchair by the shaded lamp
or stooping to throw more logs on the fire.)
These moments converge continuously. Every one is all-important
because of one common substance, because it reflects
the growth from unseen roots of everything in me
that I am today.

5
Well, dusk has ripened and total darkness has fallen.
It is hard to distinguish the edges of trees from the
background air.
How glad I am that you are here with me. You will sit now in an armchair
made of moss.
Soon everyone will come, the fire will burn more brightly,
we will drink tea and eat buttered biscuits
with jam, then we will sing . . .
How good it is that you are in the world,
because I thought you no longer were, and then I thought, I cannot reach,
yet I have reached you and feel that I have you now.

3. Father, Be My Way, Be My Source!

ADAM

The next day we had to walk through a thicket. At the edge of the forest,
where the magnificent high pine trees end,
and with them the shadows; where the pine trees end,
and with them the litter of needles and moss; where the soft
brushwood ends and a clearing begins lies
the tangle of bushes and shoots through which one forces one's way
while gathering raspberries or blackberries.
Our way takes us there.
But it is not enough to look from the outside. You must enter.

You know the thicket that is *in me:* how many people
can believe that none of us
is closed and unchangeable? We only carry in us
the content that outgrows us in its absolute form,
but we are attached to and dependent on it.
Is it true
that fatherhood is only a burden one bears alone—
not a privilege one enjoys by oneself?
And now you: you walk with me. *The child's sanctuary—*
who has the right to enter it? Surely the father has
such a right. But I only indicate the Great Meaning.
You are very shy. That is not yet simplicity,
though you are also simple: when you cannot express something,
when you are ashamed of your feelings, you know how to cry in secret.
You know also how to bring a bunch of flowers and put it on my desk when no one can see.
Your views are hermetic and grow from first impressions.
You find it hard to stand outside—and so you often feel a stranger,
even among friendly people. You adapt yourself with effort.

You are very ambitious, too; you are dependable to the point of willfulness;
I look at your features, at the way they are formed. I look at the
impenetrable sanctuary of a child. You have been lulled to sleep by the overabundance of nature,
which harmonizes with insufficiency in man.
I still remain lonely.
Suddenly a rustle wakes me. *I am not lonely, for I tremble.*
A glistening, patterned body throbs in the grass,
pulsating with measured breathing. On the beaten trail
a viper
rapidly curls up and puts out its tongue.
Obviously something has vexed it.
I am not lonely, for I tremble.
My whole awareness throbs with this one meaning—viper—
that clings to it from outside.
At the same time another meaning appears, which clings from within:
child. One must protect this child!
I am immensely moved. I know now that something has happened.
But I do not yet know exactly what.

MONICA

I know that fear has left me. You have taken it all upon yourself.
We are walking toward the forest; I am holding you by the hand, as I have held no one before . . .
The viper disappeared in the grass somewhere; you must have saved my life.
What are you thinking about?

ADAM

I was thinking about your father. He gave you life.

MONICA

Didn't you give me a new life?

ADAM

No. I only took from you
what is His due. Only in your imagination can I be linked
with the idea of the Father. I can be only for you
that Great Meaning . . . Am I able now to give you birth again?
This is the framework.

MONICA

Fill it; fill it with yourself! You must fill it with yourself!
Do you know how I need you, how much I took from you and am still taking?
But my need for you is not the reason. I want to love without any need,
aiming directly with my heart at a meaning that is both simple and great
and in which man is contained, being unable to contain it in himself.

ADAM

I know you do not love out of need—but we follow the traces of the Meaning
that is both great and simple. Can I give birth to you now?
Can you be born of me?
Only an association remain
(though life returns continually to the same old places,
it does not find us there anymore . . .).
Ah, Child, how deeply painful it is that I cannot give you birth anew—
even though you would not then be who you are now.
And for you
I can trace only from outside that Great Meaning
that we long for with all our human nature,
especially from a certain moment. . .
"Father, father"—with what Meaning
does this word resound?

MONICA

Has not the moment come yet when it could resound
for me with you and for you with me?

ADAM

We keep walking. A stream is running by; we go uphill, upstream.
Among the pine trees nearby, one can immerse one's feet in the water. Do it.
The stream is cool; the water falls quietly down the stones,
its murmur slowly grows all along its run.

MONICA

I am putting my feet in the water. What a soothing coolness, what freshness, what rebirth!
Life enters anew into all my cells.
Ah, as I am being born anew from this forest stream,
I ask: Be water for me!
I ask: Be water for me!

CHORUS

1

We have come down to the cool stream that runs in the shadow of the pine trees
nearby.
No one will recognize our footprints. Water is not stone,
nor is it clay, in which your feet leave an imprint.
Has water left its imprint on you—
or only coolness and a stillness of the body?

2

We have come down to the cool stream, which
on the gentle mountain slope and in the stately shadow of the pines
has carved out its own bed.
The bank of the stream is both the edge of the earth and the edge of human thought—

the sight flows here into objects, small trees, and stones at the
bottom.

ADAM

3

We have come down to the forest stream to praise you, the
water
that has given birth to man anew, yet we have passed by
unaware
of your own goodness.
I praise you, cool forest water, for having saved for me the
breath
that I feel so close to my heart: the breath of a child by my side.

MONICA

I will not move from this place; from this child's place I will
never move.
I want to embrace you with all my childhood, which you once
traced on the pages of an album . . . Then came the girlish
years . . .
I love you for all the yesterdays that did not happen—
and for today, in which yesterday is contained.

ADAM

Well, can we contain it? . . . How shall I find your childhood
years
in what is now? I will miss them greatly.
All the past converges at this point—suddenly, suddenly the
years come back . . .
You cannot return to them, but they can swell and come again,
flooding your heart. Child, child. How can we enter that flood?
I would enter—with great trepidation—the whole past that
moves toward us
and floods the present moment . . . I would lead you like a little
girl,
by the hand. I would then go back and separate by year

everything that is here all at once. How can all this be embraced?

MONICA

4
We have come down to the forest stream. Tell me,
are we not here at the lowest point of some strange gravitation?
How can I embrace you with all my child's being?

ADAM

Look once more: the stream—you are entering the water, which keeps falling down from here.
Through the stream do you not reach the SOURCE where everything begins?
Through the stream do you not embrace the SOURCE?

MONICA

Through the stream the SOURCE EMBRACES ME TOO.

4. The Father and the Child Embrace One Another by Means of the Word "Mine"

ADAM

. . . my child. When I first decided to think of you as my child,
by that very fact I accepted the meaning of the word "mine."
What happened? . . .
Something
quite simple yet eternal.
Some words carry weight,
even small words . . . Such is the word "mine."
With this word I accept as my own, but at the same time I give myself
. . . MY CHILD! My child! "Mine" means "own."

MONICA

I do not know how it happened, but I think this word emerged
on the waves of my heart.
The waves of the heart flow over us often in ebbs and tides—
I have felt a wave rise and fall again.
I have even feared sometimes that it would push me over, but now
I am not afraid anymore; I am used to it.
But I like stillness best—
when a huge wave, dormant in its depths,
stands still between the banks of my being.
It is better when the wave is quiet, and only I know it's there,
for when it moves, I feel again like a reed or bulrush
and feel less strongly the banks of my being.
The banks grow distant then.
Some frontiers break too and in me
strange beings roll, also uncertain of their frontiers.
I dream of a stillness so great that even those strange beings
could emerge on the wave of my heart as if they were my own.
I dream of a great stillness where nothing would disturb
the sense of all that is contained in the word "mine."

ADAM

The word "mine"—a tiny, simple word. How long I had to stand
on its threshold. How long I looked into it through all the logic
of existence . . . This word has an eternal sense . . .
Do you know that we must not accept what emerges only
on the wave of heart until we assume responsibility
for the truth of this word, the common simple word "mine"?
We may return to the heart once we have dealt
with the logic of words. How many of us fear we shall not then find again
the warm current the wave of heart carries?

Never act like a blind man who only touches objects
but devises no picture of them. Such a life would be a poor one.

And yet I do not want to belittle anything you treasure.
I shiver at the very thought that I could upset
or undermine something in you . . .
But what emerges on the wave of the heart
should not develop haphazardly, leading into blind alleys.
Every feeling, my child, must be permeated by light,
so that one does not feel in darkness, but in the light, anew.
One must transfix feelings with thought.
(I transform the delicate heart of hearts in which I stay more and more freely;
I live there as if it were my own. How many doors has she opened for me?
And if she knew of another, hidden, gate, still closed to me,
she would try at once to open it . . . yet she is not one of those who open themselves easily . . .)

MONICA

When I think of you as mine, I do not follow myself, only you,
and at the same time I go into myself to find you there.
When I find you, I feel joy. But if I do not find you,
I feel pain, and that is why sometimes I cry in secret . . .
What does it mean? Do I want to take you, to have you for my own?
Well, certainly I do. But I could not . . . and such
possession would even be impossible . . . I want only to pass into you always
so that you can find me in your heart and then
think "mine" about me . . . as one thinks about one's own child.

ADAM

We are born also through choice—then we are born from within,
and not at once but bit by bit . . .
So we are not born but rather become.
But at a particular moment we may not become, may not be born.

This depends on us. And that is why—bit by bit—I try to find credibility
in the word “mine.” Do you also try to find it, child?
Giving birth begins with unity and aims at unity. In this love consists.
When you were conceived and your mother was to give birth to you,
first you had to penetrate the depths of her body, then to tear yourself
out of it with the first impulse of independent life . . .
If you are to be born of your father, you must first penetrate
the depths of his will . . . This is giving birth through choice.
And to choose means to accept what makes my world,
what is in me and what is of me . . . Are you able to accept it?
For already I carry you under my heart and know that I must give you birth,
because I cannot think of you as other than mine.

MONICA

Oh, do not worry about giving birth . . . I know it is the woman who gives birth.
Do not fear what I say: how differently YOU ARE GIVING ME BIRTH!
You want to give me birth like this all the time—
to introduce me to what is
and what has not yet come to be (and if it is somehow already,
it is thanks to you). Though born once,
I am also many times unborn and want to be born many times.

ADAM

Do you know what I used to think?—Poor child, she has lost her father.
I can be for her the Great Meaning . . .
I only wanted to signify the father.
Then I did not want to find myself in you. But now I want to.
Now if I am to find you in myself, I must find myself in you.

Do you know that if I do this, you are not altogether free?
For love denies freedom of will to him who loves—
love liberates him from the freedom
that would be terrible to have for its own sake.
So when I become a father, I am conquered by love.
And when you become a child, you too are conquered by love.
At the same time I am liberated from freedom through love,
and so are you;
at last I am liberated from loneliness,
which I do not want to exchange for love.
Child, child. When I become father, I must want
that strange being—
subtle and timid,
bold and carefree,
cheerful and sad,
defiant and immensely vulnerable—to become mine;
I must want that strange being,
you, to be mine.
I must want her to be born of me and ever to grow out of me,
not to be born apart and grow away from me—
I must want this and tremble for it.
I must tremble too because she, being born of me,
will not for an instant cease to be herself.
Thus I have to split and divide myself from herself always,
having both myself in her and her in myself.

And if I have to tremble, that means love for a long time
has met with fear.
Love is always a choice and is always born by choice.
(This is the mystery of the word "mine.")
If I love, I must always choose you in me,
so I must always give you birth and always be born in you.
Giving birth this way through perpetual choice, we give birth to love.
(This is the mystery of the simple word "mine.")

So you see that you cannot be free any more than I.

And you too, like me, must be liberated from freedom through love.
For there is no giving birth without everything that is contained in the word "mine."
And though I would very much wish to stop at the edge, love will draw me in . . .
Do you understand this?

5. Father and Child Always Find One Another by Means of the Word "Mine"

MONICA

I cried this morning. I know that my father is sad too.
I feel this sadness very much. Why does it have to be so?
I cried; I was helpless. Can I always want
what he does when I simply want what I want?

ADAM

My child, beloved child. I cannot spare you tears.
Sometimes I even wait for them. Then I wipe them
and say, "Do not cry." What remains is to await a new maturity,
a new unity of will, a common rhythm . . .
I never doubt you, remember, but test you in myself always.

One must desire together. One cannot escape by desiring,
for then the feeling deceives . . . and the word "mine" remains in a void
and hurts because of that . . . for the void of love is the most painful:
when we love, a common current runs through our wills.
From it a certainty grows, and freedom is born again from certainty.
And this is what love means. And then without fear I think "mine" . . .

MONICA

Many times father repeated (the autumn abounded in strange tensions),
"Too many of the bonds between us are external;
there are too few inner bonds. Ah, child, I know this well —
you live too little *in me*, though you are so close."
I said then, "Is it not true that I took from you
so much? Can one take more?"

But those were difficult days. Did I misunderstand you, or could you not find me?
I decided the fault was mine.
After all, my father, you may look for me
first in yourself, and only later in me.
So I said, "It is my fault; it is my fault only"
(those were December days, which always end so quickly,
turning into evenings almost without dusk),
as if you wanted to say, It is our fault; it is ours. —It is only mine!

From now on shall I live in you?
It seems to me that you are determined, that you demand radical changes.
Sometimes it is as if you said, I must have been late in you . . . But I know
that it is I who am late. Yes, it is certainly I who am late.
You are patient, however . . .

ADAM

When we descend from word to will, what will the word mean? . . .
The meaning in that brief word "mine" is irrevocable.
I feel that one cannot turn back; one can only find
or suffer.
There was a moment, like a flash,
when I wanted to tear out of myself the meaning of the word "father."

It was only a moment. I knew you would come back. I will clear the way for you myself.
You will come back and find in me all you have desired,
and all that you are sometimes afraid of . . . Is it not true that in the word "father"
there is also fear?
I will *never* be only stillness but also storm.
Nor will I be sweetness only; I will add bitterness.
And though I try to be transparent, I will also be a puzzle.
And you will not always rest; sometimes you will be tired because of me,
my child. . .
Am I truly in you?
Is my world also your world?
Or do you enjoy feeling only on the surface—
the gentle, warm wave flowing through your heart—
and do you not even think
that from that wave you must fish out the whole inner world,
the world I call mine?
The levels of emotion can, after all, slide past each other,
touching whole people, leaving them behind . . .

There are hours, sleepless nights,
during which I grapple with the feeling
that you are created outside me, that I do not give you birth . . .
The pain of birth is a joy, but the pain of not giving
birth to a child must be terrible! . . .
There are such hours. Forgive me for them!
Maybe they too serve love.
And do not think for a moment that I would want only myself in you.
I want you so much, so much,
but always find that secret formula
through which I shall be in you,
and you in me!

MONICA

Are those not the same hours, the same sleepless nights
during which I also cry, my eyes full of tears.
Why do you sometimes appear so distant, though you are closest to me?
I realize that you cannot want me to remain outside the truth of your existence;
I realize this more and more.

ADAM

Gradually I learn through you what it means to be a father:
it means having the strongest bonds with the world . . . So let us shape that world together!
How precise we must be here, how sensitive and subtle!
But on the other hand: a slight scratch, tiny wounds that hurt a long time,
then the long healing, then the gentle cure—
understanding, and again determination that seems like vehemence . . .
but a father finds it very hard to lose, cross out, reject, and cut off
(ah, what a hope in this; what trust begins from here!).
A father finds it very hard to lose, to push out of the field of love!
Fatherhood binds me not only to the child;
it binds me also to myself: I am bound within myself.
And I find it very hard to lose myself in myself. It is not possible.
If one loses faith in one's own fatherhood (think, child), then only pain is possible.
But I cannot now cease to be myself together with what binds me from within—
my burden and happiness—because it has somehow become myself too.

MONICA

Father, father, I am here! We have come back from the
mountains.
It is lovely. The tents drying in the sun.
Resin drips down the bark, tall grass, a path runs across,
hardly, hardly trodden in the grass. A man can hide
and muse. Discover the depths of other beings and his own—
discover, reach. Reach with what is in me that which is in You.
I am, I am! Please forgive me. I want to be always.
You must not doubt this. Only sometimes I do not know how.
Do I not want to? . . . When I do not know how, do I not want
to?
No, do not think so! Never think so!

A path through high grass, hardly, hardly trodden . . .
Your child is here. You see, she will evade the vicious viper.
Your child has presence of mind, senses your world.
But she does not drink fully of that world.
Is this not well, my father? In you there must always be more;
in you there must always be something more . . .

And then pine trees—the pyramids of shade, the low bushes full
of berries,
and the stream.
I walk into the water up to my ankles, up to my knees, up to my
hips.
I feel its coolness (I touch the stones underwater);
I feel its coolness, and at the same time—
ah, Father!—
I feel, I feel my body anew
and my soul!
You took me by the hand then
and guided me.
It is not possible now to change that in you and me.
I know. And you know, too. And the rest will come.

Part III. Mother

1. Concern for Inner Radiance

MOTHER

Do not go away, child—you eternal child—never go away. Even if you depart, remember that you remain in me. All who depart remain in me. And all who pass by have their place in me—not just a wayside stop but a permanent place. I gather the people whom Adam has dispersed. There is in me a love stronger than loneliness. That love is not of me. Though I intend to speak of it, silence here expresses more than speech.

People inhabit an earth that has two poles. They have no permanent place here. They are all on their way, which leads them from the pole of loneliness to the pole of love. I love Adam and constantly restore to him the fatherhood he renounces. I discreetly turn his loneliness into my motherhood. And this is how people liberate themselves from the heritage that forms the strangest community—the community of loneliness. Adam, too, liberates himself from it. I help him leave the circle that binds him to himself.

Do not think that I inspire him. I am too simple and too tired for that. I am tired of people, as he is, but in a different way. Adam does not see my beauty, perhaps does not even know who I am. I entered his history unobserved. Among the many servants of history I am the least obtrusive. And I am not the light for those I enlighten but rather a shade in which they rest. A mother ought to be the shade for her children. A father knows he is in them: he wants to be in them and confirms himself in them. But I do not know whether I am in them—I only feel them in me. And so my absence alternates with Adam's presence, while his absence alternates with my presence. We are present and absent in different ways. If Adam knew all about me, if he knew the whole truth about me, he would cease to be embedded in loneliness and see in himself the features of the Bridegroom, which he is trying to hide.

When I give birth to children, they are not only mine but also his. Thus I restore to him at least a shadow of the fatherhood that he has renounced from the beginning, unable to renounce it altogether. And I stay in this shadow—unobserved by him, unloved. Sometimes he meets me and asks about the pain of childbirth. But he denies what I reply: our truths cannot meet. I am not the bride of him whom I love. I am only a mother.

[The upper area of the space in which the MOTHER *is standing gradually lights up. One can see people grouped as during* ADAM'S *monologue]*

People who have departed, who have fallen in so many battles—for life is full of battles—are born anew in me. I am their shelter for they do not have the full beauty from without, only the need for rest. And I do not know how it happens that I fill these people with radiance from within. Or rather I do know, but my knowledge is faith. Faith is also knowledge—although in its most sensitive point it is not knowledge any more but expectation. And this is the only radiance I can afford. I instill that radiance in people who are born of me. It is the true inner radiance coupled with outward fatigue.

I give birth to people through the fatigue that fills life as well as through the light that they experience from within. I do not give birth to them physically, as a woman, though the labor of my childbirth is no less acute—only different—for it is difficult to join fatigue with light and light with fatigue. Ah, Adam! Why does he scorn that labor? Why won't he believe in the light joined to fatigue, instead of always choosing loneliness? People born of him live in inner darkness, without expectations. I am the other pole of Adam's loneliness. I must constantly clothe his children in light because they walk naked from within. They clothe themselves on the outside with an immense wealth of creatures and of their own work, but on the inside they are naked. Yet they are ashamed. So they run away, shouting, "I have hidden away because I am naked."

I know so many women who give birth in pain. Human motherhood is branded with pain. With pain man pays for the joy of existence. A child is born naked. When its mother recovers from the pangs of labor, she bathes it, washing the tiny body to restore its freshness. I take part in all mothers' cares, and I desire to bathe every child of this earth, to wash it in water so that it remains always fresh; we must clothe it on the inside in the radiance that liberates it from the shame of existence. I ask you, mothers, to take part in my motherhood.

[Some women emerge from different groups and approach the MOTHER, *who now addresses the Invisible Child resting in her arms]*

My little one, I know now that you are alive, because you cry and laugh in turn. But I do not yet know that your cry and your laughter are heard throughout the universe. My little one, I want to spare you the shame of existence, and that is why I say, "Take into yourself the light that will guide you through Adam's loneliness and lead you to the Father." This is also the moment of my birth, the moment in which I become a Mother.

2. Radiation and Dying

ADAM

Although I am always far away from you, still I am near. So listen to me as I listen to you.

I admire the Bridegroom, yet I cannot transform myself into him. How full of human substance He is! He is the living denial of all loneliness. If I knew how to implant myself in Him, if I knew how to live in Him, I would find in myself the love that fills Him. Love reveals the Father in the Son. How much he strives for every human being—as for the greatest treasure, as someone in love strives for his beloved . . .

MOTHER

Whenever a child is born, I find you anew, Adam. It is you yourself who are born then, and I come forward to meet you with the light I want to kindle from within. I approach quietly, discreetly, so that you do not hear my steps, and each time I tell you, "Adam, accept the radiation of fatherhood; Adam, become a child." And each time you are silent. You do not hear my voice, or rather you do not want to hear. You regard me as an intruder. Sometimes you wish to drive me away, though I come each time with love. I love you in every newborn child, and through him I take you in my arms. You have become a child anew because I am near. The radiation of fatherhood passes through me, acts through my motherhood. And you, who have lost the clear vision of the Father, choosing your loneliness anew in every newborn child, must reconcile yourself with me. I am near. I am everywhere. I do not know myself how it happens, but this is so. I join the birth of every man, and through it I constantly meet you, opposing you every time. Oh, Adam, how tired I am of you. Truly, fatigue is the measure of our love—and through patience we come into possession of our souls. You must be surprised at my mindfulness of every beck and call of your kind. Do not be surprised, Adam!

How does it happen that I see the father in you, even though you reject fatherhood? That I see the child in you, even though you do not want to be one? I am afraid I always come at the call of the Bridegroom, though you never call me with His voice. I hear that voice which brings me nearer to you, even though it is not you who speaks. You want so much to be lonely that the words "sister" and "Bride" are strangers to your lips. Yet I am she. I constantly watch over the quiet flow of life in you; I constantly bend over it: my substance is the life I give you, though I do not take it from you. And you know about it.

You know where there is life, there must be a bride, a mother. I am she. This you cannot contain, but you must be contained in it. My tiny son, who is also my father: love always outgrows you but never leaves you. You do not want to be a bridegroom, yet I speak to you the words of a bride. You do not want to be a child, yet I keep giving birth to you. You do not want to be a father, because you choose loneliness, but I come to take it away from you. Love that outgrows cannot cut itself off from its soil. The soil of our love is every man. But it is the Father who is the Way and the Source.

I gather in me the RADIATION OF FATHERHOOD—and the dying of fatherhood:

When a child is born, you are born in it anew, and I rejoice in that birth. At the same time—Adam, Adam—*I desire you to die in it.* I desire your death, and in that wish I find the very nucleus of life. Because of that wish, you bear a grudge against me, and that is why you cannot understand my love for you. It is a love that outgrows you, and I keep coming back to you with that love: to you and your children *I return with the Bridegroom's death.*

You resist it.

My Bridegroom does not want to remain lonely in his death!

ADAM

All this I know. But is it enough to know? I choose loneliness to remain myself and nobody else. This is what my world is created from.

Do I really remain myself?

Our world is perpetually being created around us: my world that is our world and our world that is my world. Even as that world develops, it disintegrates. It lacks what might profoundly unite it, but in it is my loneliness. Do we not have to envisage the possibility of a total disintegration of our world?

MOTHER

I gather the radiation of Fatherhood and the dying of fatherhood: in me they are one.

[She stretches out her arms as if taking the Invisible Child into them and carrying it before her]

Who is this child?

[The people standing around them light the candles they hold: are they a procession of MOTHER *and Bride—or* ADAM'S *children?]*

ADAM

[Looks at what is happening but speaks as if he were taking no part in it, as if he wanted, above the head of the MOTHER *and her retinue, to establish contact with the Father]*

Yes, it could happen in the end that You will put aside our world. You may let it crumble around us and, above all else, in us; then it will transpire that You remain whole only in the Son, and He in You, and whole with Him in Your Love. Father and Bridegroom. And everything else will then turn out to be unimportant and inessential except this: father, child, and love.

And then, looking at the simplest things, we will all say, Could we not have learned this long ago? Has this not always been embedded in everything that is?

[He speaks these last words as if he wanted to hand them down to the people standing around. Indeed they repeat the words after him]

CHORUS

Could we not have learned this long ago?
Has this not always been embedded in everything that is?

[A moment's silence, broken by the MOTHER'S *voice]*

MOTHER

You are wrong, Adam! You are all wrong!

In me will survive the heritage of all men, implanted in the Bridegroom's death.

REFLECTIONS ON FATHERHOOD

by Fr. Karol Wojtyła (Pope John Paul II), 1964

translated by Bolesław Taborski

Ex quo omnis paternitas in coelis
et in terra nominatur.

For many years now I have lived like a man exiled from my deeper personality yet condemned to probe it.

During those years I have toiled unceasingly to reach it, always thinking with horror that it was becoming lost, blurred among the mass processes of history.

Not for nothing am I called Adam. In this name one can meet every man; at the same time in this name everything that man contributes can be made ordinary. That is what I thought through all those years; I thought that my footsteps should be wiped out, that I had to obliterate myself so that I could identify with the average man, whose history is written from without by a mobilized crowd. What else does the name ADAM mean?

Do you want to substitute for it something from within? But what? Should one not recoil from it with terror?

Although I am like the man who can be placed apart and then made a common denominator for all men, I still remain lonely.

Nobody calls this loneliness a sin, but I know what to make of it. And I know who Adam is, he who stopped once on the frontier between the promise of fatherhood and his own loneliness. Who cut him off from men? Who made him lonely in the midst of them all? After all, he became lonely of his own free will in order to graft that loneliness onto others. Who will not call that a fault?

He is lonely. I asked myself, What will bring me nearer to Him than loneliness? What will make me more like Him, that is to say, more independent of everything?

If, having formed me of clay, You had said, Clay, go on forming, I would have formed many a thing. You know best the staggering temperatures of kilns where clay is baked—You for whom the entire computation of atoms is the simplest intuition, not a compilation of figures and formulas. I would surely pluck out many more things from Your intelligence and implant them in my world—calling It is I, it is I, that is true—but that world would be Yours, anyway. For what am I? . . . I, who am transient all the time.

Did You have to touch my thought with Your birth giving and my will with the love that fulfills itself in Him and at the same time is born of Him? In me it will never fulfill itself because I cannot give birth in this way. That is why You were disappointed in me. Did I not call from the start, "Leave me my loneliness"? Why did I call thus? I know I called in spite of myself, but even more in spite of You.

I am afraid of the word "mine," though at the same time I love it most and cherish best its meaning. I am afraid because this word always puts me face to face with You.

A thorough analysis of the word "mine" always leads to You. And I would rather give it up than ultimately find it in You. For I want to have everything through myself, not through You. If to want this is nonsense, still, haven't many people harnessed themselves to serve it? In the midst of a multitude are people not more and more lonely? Numbers do not engender love, and loneliness does not make people independent but rather engenders strife. What can I say after all this? Can I ask, Forgive me that I execute my plan with such obstinacy? That I am still a common denominator for everyone, which can be substituted for anyone or a common word that can be put outside the brackets? That I continually evade Your Fatherhood and gravitate toward my loneliness so that You must reveal yourself in an external vacuum?

Still You execute Your plan.

One could say You are relentless in Your determination: Your plans are irreversible. The strangest thing transpires in the end: that You are never really against me. You only force Your way into what I call loneliness, and You overcome my resistance. But do You really force Your way in or only enter through a door that is open anyway? You did not make me closed; You did not quite close me. The desire for loneliness is not at the bottom of my being at all but continually rises through a fissure of my being, a fissure much wider than I could have imagined. This is where You enter and slowly begin to enhance me from within.

You enhance me in spite of what I have imagined about my ego, yet in harmony with what I am. Can I wonder that You are stronger in me than myself? You aim at me through a child—and my resistance will be broken. Nothing will remain of the loneliness with which I have resisted You, while You will express Yourself deeply. Gradually I shall cease to feel that You express Yourself in me and begin to think that I express myself in myself. And it will be so until the moment when love hurts. It will hurt through lack of fulfillment, a lack of my ego in the beloved other ego, or the other way around . . . Yet precisely then it can best be seen that man cannot reject from his consciousness the word "mine" but must go where it leads him. And this word cancels loneliness.

After a long time I came to understand that You do not want me to be a father if I am not also a son. The son is wholly Yours; You always think "mine" about him. And You utter this word with absolute justification, with credibility. Without such credibility the word "mine" is a risk; love is a risk too. Why did You inflict on me the love that in me must be a risk? And now Your Son takes on Himself all the risk of fatherly love in relation to everything outside Himself. How much the word "mine" must hurt when what it describes turns out later not to be mine. I think with awe about the strain and toil of Your Son, about the magnitude of His love. How much did He take on Himself? What voids did He fill? How great is the void He has to fill! After all, in every one of us there remains only the common denominator in which, against all the logic of existence, "mine" continually tries to force out "Yours."

How could I become a son? I did not want to be him. I did not want to accept the suffering caused by risking love. I thought I would not be equal to it. My eyes were too fixed on myself, on my ego and its possibilities alone.

When Your Son came, I remained the common denominator of man's inner loneliness. Your Son wanted to enter it. He wanted to because He loves. Loneliness opposes love. On the borderline of loneliness, love usually becomes suffering. Your Son suffered. He suffered because in all of us there is that common denominator of untransformed loneliness, and for You, Father, that loneliness is opposed to the simple substance that You express with the word "mine."

Who could wish that the truth contained in that word should transform our loneliness? Could I, who gave birth to that loneliness, have wished it? Only He could have wanted it—Your Son.

To absorb the radiation of fatherhood means not only to become a father but, much more, to become a child (become a son). Being the father of many, many people, I must be a child: the more I am a father, the more I become a child.

Though I look at the Son with admiration, yet I cannot transform myself into Him. How full of human substance He is! He is the living denial of all loneliness. If I knew how to immerse myself in Him, if I knew how to implant myself in Him, I would find in myself the Love that fills Him. It is the love that reveals the Father in the Son and in the Father, through the Son, gives birth to the Bridegroom. Father and Bridegroom: how much He strives for every human being—as for the greatest treasure, a unique good; as someone in love strives for his beloved: the Bridegroom and the Son. All this I know. But is it enough to know? Knowing, I can continue to substitute for everything the same old common denominator of my loneliness—my inner loneliness, chosen so that I can remain myself alone and nobody else. From this my world is created. If it is also "our" world, then all its works and products are permeated with the climate of "my" loneliness too—and so it is in all of us. That world develops, or seems to, but at the same time it disintegrates. For it lacks that which profoundly unites, something that would enter it and unify all its elements. So we have to envisage the possibility of a total disintegration of that world of ours, whose works and products are permeated with our loneliness, our common loneliness.

And in the end You could put aside our world. You may let it crumble around us and, above all else, in us. And then it will transpire that YOU remain whole only in the SON, and He in You—whole with Him in YOUR LOVE, Father and Bridegroom.

And everything else will then turn out to be unimportant and inessential, except for this: father, child, and love.

And then, looking at the simplest things, all of us will say: could we not have learned this long ago? Has this not always been embedded at the bottom of everything that is?

[1964]

ON STAGE

New Words for Ancient Truths

by Kenneth L. Schmitz

Chapter 1: *At the Center of the Human Drama: The Philosophical Anthropology of Karol Wojtyła/Pope John Paul II.*

The present pope has caught the imagination of many throughout the world—Christians or not. And he has done it by playing out the drama inherent in the world's oldest elective office, often in new ways. From the Chair of Peter he has poured his energies above all into the task of universal teacher, the voice at the center of the Catholic Church; his actions for the most part flow out of that teaching. It has been his intention to build up the Church from within, by word and deed; but it is clearly also his hope to stand with Christ at the center of the events that shape all mankind. The formative elements of his instruction and action can be traced as they have grown out of the intuitions of a rather remarkable young man from Wadowice. I purpose in these lectures to sketch some of those elements and that formation—simplifying by necessity, if not out of ignorance, but attempting to stay near the main lines of development, especially with regard to his philosophical ideas. For they have articulated his religious sensibilities and contributed to his theological reflections.

Although the central intuitions matured in their proper time, they seem already to have received a certain shape and impetus when in 1939 the young Karol Wojtyła set about his higher studies at the Jagiellonian University—Copernicus's university—in Cracow. For he took up the study of Polish letters, language, and history. As you know, the period 1940–45 coincided with some of the darkest years of that nation's dark yet glorious history. Wojtyła's interest leaned toward the record of that history as it was given expression by poets and national heroes. The dramatic energy of his later works and deeds no doubt found early expression in this interest. He did not fail to notice the interplay of word and deed in that national record. But his religious interest was caught also by an older history—biblical history. His first works for the theater gave dramatic expression to the blending of themes played out in those different histories. In these first dramatic works and in a time of great national suffering, he forged a convergence that deliberately overrode the difference in times between the events in ancient Israel, those in Poland's past, and the terrible events during the dreadful Nazi occupation.

A first play, no longer extant, was entitled *David.*[1] The second (Spring 1940) took up the theme of *Job*, and the third (Summer 1940) that of *Jeremiah*, sub-titled *A National Drama in Three Acts*. I have the impression that in Polish culture, as in some other cultures, more perhaps than in our own, the word has a special weight. It may be the particular genius of the language, or because the language was the last bastion the nation could fall back upon in defense of its cultural identity—I do not know. What is certain, at any rate, is that the young Wojtyła was fascinated by the word—spoken, written, and declaimed. Less than a month after the end of hostilities and the beginning of the occupation of his native land, he wrote to a fellow thespian: "Let theater be a church where the national spirit will flourish."[2]

Wojtyła worked at this time in a quarry (and later in a chemical plant) while he pursued his university studies covertly. During this time he joined forces with Mieczysław Kotlarczyk in a clandestine theater of the "living word." Gathered in cramped domestic quarters in the sparse conditions of occupied Poland, the Rhapsodic Theater Company (as it came to be known) produced seven plays during the years 1941 to 1944, gave twenty-two performances, and held over a hundred rehearsals under the most dangerous conditions. Of this time, Wojtyła was later to remark: "Of all the complex resources of the theatrical art, there remained only the living word, spoken by people in extrascenic conditions, in a room with a piano. That unheard-of-scarcity of the means of expression turned into a creative experiment."[3]

---

1. For a more detailed discussion of Wojtyła's early theatrical activity—as dogsbody, actor, prompter, director, playwright—and his continuing interest in the theater, see the introduction by Bolesław Taborski (ed.) in Karol Wojtyła, *The Collected Plays and Writings on Theater* (Berkeley: U of California Press, 1987), pp. 1-16; hereafter, *CP*.

2. Quoted by Taborski, in *CP*, p. 5, from a letter of the nineteen-year-old Wojtyła to Mieczysław Kotlarczyk, written on Nov. 2, 1939, in which he urged Kotlarczyk to come to Cracow in order to form a theater company.

3. "Drama of Word and Gesture" (1957) (*CP*, p. 379).

A theater critic has referred to the Rhapsodic Theater as "a theater of the imagination, a theater of the inner self."[4] Even after the war, Wojtyła's own plays continued to employ severe staging, symbolic background music and dance, and a chorus that gives emphasis to the ethical implications at decisive points;[5] but all of these extra-verbal accoutrements are subordinated to the inner discipline of the word and its meaning. Indeed, he distinguishes the theater of the word from more traditional theater by the different roles played out by the word in each: "The position of the word in a theater is not always the same. As in life, the word can appear as an integral part of action, movement, and gesture, inseparable from all human practical activity; or it can appear as 'song'—separate, independent, intended only to contain and express thought, to embrace and transmit a vision of the mind."[6]

In traditional theater, the word accompanies the other elements which surround it as part of the total theatrical action, whereas in the theater of the word it is the word that frames the whole. And it is the word that draws out of its own meaning whatever movement, gesture, and background complements its expression. That is why, as far as possible, the staging and music, and every gesture of actor, chorus or dance group, turns upon and synchronically with the turn of the words. Whereas traditional theater tells a story through the impact of event upon character, the theater of the word sets forth a problem, an issue of import: "The problem itself acts, rouses interest, disturbs, evokes the audience's participation, demands understanding and a solution."[7] The word and its meaning "mature in spare, simple, rhythmic gesture," and the movement, sounds, and staging arise out of the reservoir of meaning

4. Marta Bojarska, a contemporary drama critic; cited by Taborski, *CP*, p. 7—In *The Jeweler's Shop* (1960), act 3, scene 4 (*CP*, p. 316), Monica imagines her forthcoming wedding day "like rehearsals in a theater: the theater of my imagination and the theater of my thought."

5. In "Rhapsodies of the Millennium" (1958) (*CP*, p. 386), Wojtyła remarks: "The Rhapsodic Theater asks young actors to subordinate themselves to the great poetic word. This can be felt particularly when the word is developed in immaculately spoken choruses. A group of people collectively, somehow unanimously, subordinated to the great poetic word, evoke ethical associations; this solidarity of people in the word reveals particularly strongly and accentuates the reverence that is the point of departure for the rhapsodists' work and the secret of their style."

6. "On the Theater of the Word" (1952) (CP, p. 372).

7. Ibid. (*CP*, p. 373).

contained in the words and in the problem they articulate. To be sure, the drama of the word is frankly intellectual: "The new proportions between word and movement, between word and gesture, doubtless reach even further, in a sense beyond theater and into the philosophical concept of man and the world. The supremacy of word over gesture indirectly restores the supremacy of thought over movement and impulse in man."[8]

Such a theatrical presentation is not static, however, but moves rather with the dynamics of thought, and with the dynamics of the issue at stake, which "the living human word grasps and makes into a nucleus of action." The theater of the word, he tells us, "does not infringe on the realist standpoint but enables us to understand the inner base of human action, the very fulcrum of human movement."[9] Such inner dramas must draw upon concrete and relevant issues and refer them to the world of thought—and he underscores the last word: not fantasy but thought.[10] Indeed, in his last play, *Radiation of Fatherhood* (1964), which he subtitles *A Mystery*, the figure of the mother says: "At no point can the world be fiction, the inner world even less than the external world. . . . It is no metaphor, but reality (that is played out on stage). The world cannot depend on metaphor alone, the inner world even less than the external world."[11] And so the theater of the word aims at being a theater of reality—if I may so put it—at "symbolic realism."

By slowing the pace of the action and reducing the external surroundings, such a drama intends to effect a catharsis, as all drama must;

8. In "Drama of Word and Gesture" (*CP*, pp. 380-82), Wojtyła further insists that in the theater of the word, while the word is freed from externals to a large degree, it must not be divorced from thought, since thought provides the basis for the unique theatrical realism of the theater of the word.—In "On the Theater of the Word," no. 2 (*CP*, p. 375), he is careful, moreover, to distinguish the deeper symbolic realism of the theater of the word from the surface realism of naturalism.

9. "Drama of Word and Gesture" (*CP*, p. 380).

10. In "Rhapsodies of the Millennium" (1958) (*CP*, p. 383), he insists that the Rhapsodists "not only derive the word from the immediate needs of concrete life but also refer to that life from the world of thought. Not—it must be stressed—the world of fantasy, but the world of thought."

11. *Radiation*, part 1, scene 5 (*CP*, p. 341). She affirms that, as the radiation of the Fatherhood of God, creation is neither fiction nor metaphor. The primacy of truth as normative principle of reality recurs throughout the plays; but also the caution not to separate truth from love.

it is a catharsis not primarily of feeling, however, but of meaning. And indeed, at their best, Wojtyła's own dramas reach high dramatic effects. Paradoxically, such a reduced external structure permits the dramatic presentation of themes too broad for a traditional stage, even though the traditional stage is physically more spacious than the setting of the theater of the word. The traditional stage achieves marvelous effects in its own way, but it is bound inextricably to the particularities of its setting and plot, so that it proves too narrow to do justice to the large, even eternal, themes that only a drama of thought can embrace with the freedom adequate to their treatment.[12]

☙

Let us select several themes that are prominent in the dramas and important to my purpose. There can be no doubt that *Job* was composed in the first anguish of a brutal occupation, yet the script of the drama remains faithful in substance to the biblical text as its subtitle declares: *A Drama from the Old Testament.* The inscription on the title page forges the convergence of past, present, and future times under the eternal word of God:

> The Action Took Place in the Old Testament Before Christ's Coming. The Action Takes Place in Our Days In Job's Time For Poland and the World. The Action Takes Place in the Time of Expectation, Of Imploring Judgment, In the Time of Longing For Christ's Testament, Worked Out In Poland's and the World's Suffering.[13]

No doubt, then, that Poland is borne in mind as a collective Job. The Epilogue repeats what the Prologue chants: "Behold, my people—and

---

12. In "Drama of Word and Gesture" (*CP*, p. 382), he remarks: "The word, however, must not be divorced from thought. The specific base of theatrical realism discovered by Mieczysław Kotlarczyk with his company opens wide the horizons of theatrical practice to encompass works that by their nature could not otherwise be the object of theatrical production. . . . Perhaps other great works of the human mind, for instance the works of philosophers, could thus be adapted for at least some audiences."

13. *Job,* title page (*CP*, p. 25).—Already in a letter of Nov. 2, 1939, to Kotlarczyk, Wojtyła had written: "I think that our liberation ought to be a gate for Christ. I think of an Athenian Poland, but more perfect than Athens with all the magnitude of Christianity, such as our great poets imagined, those prophets of Babylonian captivity" (quoted by Taborski, in *CP*, p. 75).—For some details of the occupation, as well as later events, see the personal memoir of a friend: M. Maliński, *Pope John Paul II. The Life of Karol Wojtyła.* trans. P. S. Falla (New York: Crossroad, 1981).

listen to the Word of the Lord, you who are downtrodden, you who are flogged, sent to the camps, you—Jobs—Jobs."[14]

At the point in the biblical text, however, at which Elihu enters (Job 32), the close adherence to the biblical text breaks off. With the conclusion of the argument between Job and his erstwhile friends, the young man Elihu is seized with the spirit of prophecy and the drama turns to the vision of the coming of Christ, His passion and death: "He is coming—I know He lives. . . . I see that the Redeemer lives."[15] In place of the speeches of Yahweh in the biblical text, we hear a Voice which can be none other than that of Christ in the Garden of Gethsemane. And with that, suffering takes on a positive inner meaning.[16] As the first light of a new dawn begins to break behind the stage curtain, Elihu promises that a New Covenant shall arise from the Suffering. And the drama comes to a close with the counsel:

> Take these words against the storm; hold them when darkness descends. They will be for you like the silent lightning cutting the sky above Job.... Thus God's waves wash over us, overthrowing one, raising up another. Watch the waves—watch the waves. Nourish your heart today, brother. This is a tragedy of suffering—the sacrificial circle is closed. Depart—with a song on your lips. Depart from here—remember.[17]

ɷ

In the next drama, *Jeremiah*, the connection with Polish history is made even more explicit.[18] It is ostensibly set amid the great events of the seventeenth century, but it also resonates with the Poland of 1940 and with Jeremiah's plaint: "The city has fallen. . . . The enemies have struck Judah. . . . For the temples of Zion have been entered by the unclean band of armed heathen."[19] The theme of the primacy of truth is once again played out. We learn that to be chosen by God means to be

14. *Job*, "Prologos" (*CP*, p. 29); repeated in "Epilogos" (*CP*, p. 72).

15. *Job* (*CP*, p. 68).

16. Cf. the apostolic letter *Salvifici Dolores: On the Christian Meaning of Human Suffering* (11 Feb. 1984; Vatican trans., Boston: Daughters of St. Paul).

17. *Job*, "Epilogos" (*CP*, p. 73).

18. For helpful details regarding the historical figures and situation see Taborski, *CP*, pp. 75-91.

19. *Jeremiah*, act 3: "The Lamentations of Jeremiah" (*CP*, p. 130), broadly paraphrased in the drama after the fashion of monastic chant.

"chosen to proclaim God's truth." And, following upon the playing of the *Miserere* (Psalm 51), Jeremiah's cry is surely heard against the propaganda that filled the airwaves of 1940: "One must throw truth across the path of lies. One must throw truth into the eye of a lie."[20] For "in truth are freedom and excellence," but in untruth, only slavery.

And yet for all the importance attached to words, the seventeenth-century Jesuit priest, Father Peter Skarga Paweski, warns that "words are not enough, not enough"; he continues: "One must catch hearts to kindle them, furrow hearts as with a plough, and root up the weeds—root them out."[21] The crown Hetman, Stanisław Żołkiewski, adds, "At the feet of truth one must erect love; at the foundations, low in the ground, it will take root even in a wilderness, will build, uplift, and transform all things."[22]

☙

The postwar plays intensify and deepen the religious theme. The accent is even more consciously upon the "inner space" of the drama. The path within is meant to search out the truth about humanity in the maze of Stalinist realism with its clichés, and beyond that, to touch upon the central character's "spiritual struggles and his progress to sanctity."[23] Wojtyła tells us, however, that the intention is not to recount the psychological experiences of the characters but to follow up a line that is "inaccessible to history . . . an extrahistorical element in man lies at

---

20. *Jeremiah*, act 1 (*CP*, pp. 101-3, 109).

21. *Jeremiah*, act 1 (*CP*, p. 98); act 2 (*CP*, p. 121).

22. *Jeremiah*, act 2 (*CP*, p. 121), adding: "In your speeches you call for truth. . . ." To which Father Peter replies: "A call of despair is in my speeches. Mine is not a voice of revelation. . . ." This is a reference to Father Peter's jeremiad against the injustices of his day and the prophecy that Poland would fall because of them. In act 3 (*CP*, p. 137), he warns: "The ship sways but still sails on impressively," but "worms already hatching, though, eat her from within." And yet the drama sounds a note of hope. The Hetman speaks (*CP*, p. 138): "What is beyond is God's. There man will not dare. One man cannot sway the hearts of a people. He can sow the seed, graft a seedling, but does the plant grow as man wills it to grow? It grows as God wills, for God's is the harvest."

23. Comment by Taborski, *CP*, p. 152.—In his own introduction to *Our God's Brother*, Wojtyła remarks (*CP*, p. 159) that "this will be an attempt to penetrate the man . . . the fact of humanity—and concrete humanity at that."

the very sources of his humanity."[24]

The third extant play, *Our God's Brother* (1945-50; published in 1979, first staged in 1980), is a study of Adam Chmielowski (1845-1916), a partisan fighter and an artist, who later as Brother Albert worked with the poor of Cracow and founded congregations of religious brothers and sisters dedicated to that work.[25] The forces of the drama swirl about and within Adam.

A major topic of conversation in the circle around Adam addresses the question of the social responsibility of art. A colleague protests against subjectivism in art because it betrays the true nature of artistic creation: "For in reality something slowly grows around you (during the process of artistic creation), gathers momentum, widens. Of course, though you have a part in it, you are not the only originator of this mystery. That much is clear." And indeed, some of the circle consider Adam to be a seeker who is drawn out of himself.[26] Adam remains unconvinced, however, at least as it applies to his own artistic work. Instead, he sees his painting as a means of running away from something or someone indefinable.[27]

---

24. From Wojtyła's own introduction to *Our God's Brother* (*CP*, p. 159). This does not mean that one abstracts from the historical situation of the characters, but only that a human being is not exclusively historical. In this search, one arrives at probability: "Probability, however, is always an expression of the truth one has searched for; what matters is how much real truth it contains. And that depends on the intensity and integrity of the search." The aim is "to participate in the same multifarious reality in which [the character] participated—and in a way similar to him."—In *Forefathers' Eve and the Twentieth Anniversary* (1961), referring to the Rhapsodic Theater, Wojtyła insists that the drama's inwardness is not an "epic of introspection," and that "the drama does more than analyze [the heroes'] experiences and recreate the stream of their 'dramatic consciousness'" (*CP*, p. 390).

25. He was canonized by the pope in 1983.—For a correlation of the various characters in the drama with Chmielowski and his circle, see Taborski, *CP*, pp. 147-57 and footnotes.

26. *Our God's Brother*, act 1 (*CP*, p. 169): ". . . a typical seeker. Not one who rummages for petty things, but a vigorous, even boisterous seeker."

27. ". . . something, or rather someone, in oneself and in all those people" (*Our God's Brother*, act 1 [*CP*, pp. 182-83]). Adam protests that "something in me keeps opening up . . . it's chasing me." It is a painful, "gradual elucidation," which a theologian friend thinks may be a vocation; yet when Adam asks, "To what?" the reply is given, "I don't know. You must keep running away." Cf. Francis Thompson's *The Hound of Heaven*: "I fled Him, down the nights and down the days; / I fled Him, down the arches of the years; / I fled Him, down the labyrinthine ways / Of my own mind. . . ."

Another painter friend, Max, defends subjectivism. He argues that it is sufficient that an artist explore his own selfhood and give it expression; if it interests others, that is beside the point. Max will admit that he has a public persona, but he dubs this public persona "the exchangeable man," since it is subject to the barter of social life. The genuine and inviolable person, he insists, is private; he dubs that persona "the non-exchangeable man," withdrawn behind the fortress façade of an inaccessible loneliness.[28] A fellow artist protests that such an attitude diminishes the meaning of art and its creative power, and the discussion continues.

Adam cannot accept the isolated loneliness advocated by Max, but neither can he be satisfied with the safe routine of social life: "Yes, we are hiding; we escape to little islands of luxury, to the so-called social life, to so-called social structure and feel secure. But no. This security is a big lie, an illusion. It blinds our eyes and stops up our ears, but it will shatter in the end."[29]

Several rather mysterious protagonists enter into the discussion. A principal character is called the Stranger, without further identification; but he seems to represent in some way the revolutionary, who counts on the anger of the poor to break open the circle of poverty in the name of justice denied.[30] Nowhere in the play is there any indication that the playwright disagrees with the justice of this anger, and in several places he has given it eloquent expression through the mouth

28. The theme of loneliness in modern life and the fragmentation of society will recur again and again in Wojtyła's later writings. Cf. *Radiation of Fatherhood* on loneliness and the theme of fragmentation in his social encyclicals.

29. In *Our God's Brother*, act 1 (*CP*, p. 179), Adam remarks: "Each of us goes his own way. Each builds his own nest. Meanwhile, for so many people the road has become too narrow. They have nowhere to stand. They have no patch of ground they can call their own, no slice of bread they can earn, no child they can bring into this world without the certainty that it will be in everybody's way. And in the midst of all this we move, arrogantly confident in the strength of a general system that makes us ignore what cries out to be heard and suppress a justified outbreak."—The whole section resonates with social comment.

30. At one point (*Our God's Brother*, act 2: "In the Vaults of Anger," scene 8: "A Collector for Charity" [*CP*, p. 230]), angered with what he takes to be Adam's sentimentality, the Stranger accuses Adam of leaving the poor doubly depraved: by their own poverty and his handout charity, so that they are robbed of the power to reclaim their dignity.

of the Stranger.[31] Adam rebukes the Stranger for exploiting the just anger of the poor, but he too recognizes the justice of that anger. Going against its grain, however, and in the name of an at-this-point unnamed love, he calls upon the poor to "Be one of us!" He also asks the poor to acknowledge a wider and deeper poverty that lies beyond the lack of material goods; it is the poverty of values. For man is meant to aspire to all goods, to the "whole vastness of the values to which man is called." And the greatest good calls not for anger but for love. *Ubi caritas, ibi Deus.*

On the other side of the discussion taking place within Adam—within his dramatic inner space—is a voice simply dubbed "The Other." The Other seems to represent in some way the mind of the Enlightenment intelligentsia. It calls Adam to a kind of human maturity. Adam, however, finds it to be a truncated sort of maturity, because it rests everything upon merely understanding the world as it is without shouldering its burdens.

At this point, Adam finds his own salvation, instead, when he helps a poor man whom he notices leaning wretchedly against a lamp post in the cold dark street. For in that man Adam comes at last to see an image. It is not an easy vision, however, and Adam struggles against the awareness that he must give himself up if he is to identify with this

31. The Stranger harangues Adam: "Ah, charity. A *złoty* here, a *złoty* there, for the right to secure the possession of the millions invested in banks, forests, land, bonds, shares . . . who knows what else. This is what it boils down to in practice. For a *złoty* here, a *złoty* there, marked and accounted for exactly—while at the same time others toil animal-like, ten, twelve, sixteen hours a day for a miserable penny, for less than the right to live, for the hope of a dubious consolation up above, a consolation that changes nothing but has for centuries fettered the mighty, magnificent eruption of human anger—creative human anger." Adam: "Is it possible that you may be right in so much that you have said? . . . But you know, all that is terrible, terrible!" (*Our God's Brother,* act 1 [*CP*, p. 192]).—"A dubious consolation up above": A union orator expresses a similar anger in George Eliot's *Felix Holt* (London: Penguin, 1866) p. 397: "They'll give us plenty of heaven. We may have land there. That's the sort of religion they like—a religion that gives us working men heaven, and nothing else. But we'll offer to change with 'em. We'll give them back some of their heaven, and take it out in something for us and our children in this world."—We find the recognition of injustice also in his papal social encyclicals and in his national addresses (such as those of his Mexican and Canadian visits). But, while he has experienced hunger, cold, and persecution, he—like Adam—has transmuted that suffering not into anger but into the reality of Christian love.

image. He cries out: "How can I cease to be who I am?"[32] Nevertheless, it is through this discovery that Adam is at last able to say, "I am not alone."[33]

The newly discovered image is not, however, the visual image to which his art has given expression, not even the image of *Ecce Homo,* the subject of his latest and best painting. It is not that art does not count. On the contrary, Adam's priest-confessor reassures him that "God regards your art with a father's eye," since it brings people nearer to God through its reflected glory. But Adam has seen a deeper image than art can shape: it is a non-pictorial image, "imperceptible to my eye but that preys upon my soul."[34] Indeed, it is clear that it is the very image of God that is struggling for recognition and realization in his own soul, and in that of the poor man. Calling out to The Other, to the voice of the Enlightenment, Adam shouts with joy over having given up "the tyranny of intelligence," of an intelligence without love, with its "clear image of the world." Instead, he has found a different, deeper, mysterious image. The Other does not or cannot understand him, however, and Adam experiences an exultant liberation: "You don't know! So there is a sphere in my thought that you do not possess."

Is it too much to see here an autobiographical undercurrent in which the drama plays out, not only the Christian response to both socialist collectivism and to Enlightenment individualism, but also Wojtyła's own renunciation of art as his principal way of life?[35] It is not that others should not pursue art as a vocation, but that Wojtyła himself was called to enter upon another path.

Near the end of the drama Adam, now Brother Albert, speaks to a postulant of a "different sort of art,"[36] the art of serving God through being one with the poor. It is an art prompted by the generosity of God,

---

32. Later (*Our God's Brother,* act 3, "The Brother's Day" [*CP*, p. 249]), a member of Brother Albert's religious community, the cook, says, "We didn't come here to have an easy time."

33. *Our God's Brother,* act 1 (*CP*, p. 185).—Cf. the image of the double tree trunk as the presence of the parent in the child (*Radiation of Fatherhood*, part 2, scene 2 [*CP*, p. 345]); also, how, as Monica enters the stream, the Source embraces her (scene 3 [*CP*, p. 351]).

34. *Our God's Brother,* act 2, scene 2 (*CP*, pp. 204-5).

35. It may be that Wojtyła had taken up the study of Polish philology as a preparation for a lifelong career in theater. See Taborski, *CP*, p. 3.

36. *Our God's Brother,* act 3 (*CP*, pp. 256ff.).

who has changed the slavery of the fall into the freedom of the Cross. As the play comes to a close, the brothers report an outbreak in the city, an outbreak of that long-repressed, just anger, an act of collective awareness turned against oppressors. Brother Albert recognizes it for what it is and that it is an anger that will last as long as injustice itself. But—and this is one of his last days in a life devoted to the poor—he says quietly, almost to himself: "I know for certain, though, that I have chosen a greater freedom."

❧

The best known of his plays, at least in English, is *The Jeweler's Shop* (published in 1960 under the pseudonym Andrzej Jawień), modestly subtitled: "A Meditation on the Sacrament of Matrimony, Passing on Occasion into a Drama."[37] The structure of the drama is interesting in itself. In addition to the Old Jeweler, the Chorus, and the Christ figure of the Bridegroom, the chief protagonists are seven: three couples and a somewhat mysterious figure, a Chance Interlocutor, who we learn is named Adam and who represents a sort of modern Everyman. He is recognized at the very end as "a common denominator of us all—at the same time a spokesman and a judge."[38] The Old Jeweler is also a shadowy figure; perhaps he speaks for Divine Providence or is the voice of conscience.[39]

The drama divides into three acts, each of which contains, for the most part, alternating monologues, as if spoken out loud but into a surrounding and receptive silence. In the first act we meet Teresa and Andrew during their courtship and impending marriage. It is a short but happy marriage, and the widowed Teresa keeps the presence of Andrew somehow alive within her after he is killed in battle. In the second act

37. Taborski (*CP*, pp. 267-75) terms it a poetic drama and suggests that the subtitle downplays the dramatic power of the work. He points also to its innovative form, and mentions similarities with Péguy, Claudel, Pinter, Eliot, and others.

38. *The Jeweler's Shop*, act 3, scene 5 (*CP*, p. 321). Curiously, without naming himself, he names each of the protagonists. And (act 3, scene 4 [*CP*, p. 318]) at the wedding he takes the place of Christopher's long-dead father, Andrew, since—as Adam himself observes—he could not die for Andrew. Adam somehow embodies the human nature common to each of us.

39. Suggested by Taborski, *CP*, p. 271.

we meet Anna and Stefan whose marriage has been broken by a mutual disillusion and anger. In the third act we meet Monica, the daughter of the separated couple, and Christopher, the son of the first couple. The young people are planning to marry. In sum, then, we have a theme: the exploration of married love in and through a brief but happy marriage, at once both sad and joyful; a failed marriage, treated sympathetically and without facile judgment; and a forthcoming marriage, trembling with fear and hope.[40] This threefold structure provides ample dramatic space for an exploration of married love. The present purpose will be best served by emphasis upon two themes among several within the drama.

The first theme explores love as the interplay between mind and reality, between consciousness and existence: these are the noetic and the ontological dimensions of love. Love is at once something intensely conscious and very real. On the one hand, love is the conscious presence of one person in and with another.[41] But it is thereby also a union in reality. The Chorus celebrates the union of the first couple: "New People—Teresa and Andrew—two until now but still not one, one from now on though still two."[42] Anna later recalls that Adam had spoken of love as "a synthesis of two people's existence, which converges, as it were, at a certain point and makes them one."[43] But the rift, the bro-

---

40. Reflecting upon her own marriage and the forthcoming marriage of the children, Teresa speaks to her absent yet somehow still-present husband: "You have no notion, my husband, how terrible the fear is that borders on hope and penetrates it daily. There is no hope without fear and no fear without hope" (*The Jeweler's Shop*, act 3, scene I [*CP*, p. 310]).—Monica, wounded by the rift in her own parents' marriage, asks, "Is human love at all capable of enduring through man's whole experience?" (act 3, scene 2 [*CP*, p. 311]). The tension between existence and love runs throughout the last two acts.

41. At the beginning of their courtship Andrew speaks of "the basis of that strange persistence of Teresa in me, the cause of her presence, the assurance of her place in my ego, or what creates around her that strange resonance . . ." (*The Jeweler's Shop*, act 1, scene 1 [*CP*, p. 281]).

42. *The Jeweler's Shop*, act 1, scene 5 (*CP*, p. 290).

43. *The Jeweler's Shop*, act 2, scene 2 (*CP*, p. 300).—When Anna, after the separation, tries to sell her wedding ring, the Old Jeweler will not accept it: "This ring does not weigh anything; the needle does not move from zero, and I cannot make it show even a milligram. Your husband must be alive, in which case neither of your rings, taken separately, will weigh anything—only both together will register. My jeweler's scales have this peculiarity, that they weigh not the metal but man's entire being and fate" (act 2, scene 2 [*CP*, pp. 297-98]).

kenness of love in Anna and Stefan, also retains these two dimensions. Anna reflects upon her separation from Stefan, a separation both in consciousness and in reality. Stefan no longer reacts to me, she says to herself: he is no longer present in me; and yet, though I now exist for myself, I am no longer at home in myself. And she ponders the pain inherent in a broken love:

> It was as if I had become unaccustomed to the walls of my interior—so full had they been of Stefan that without him they seemed empty. Is it not too terrible a thing to have committed the walls of my interior to a single inhabitant who could disinherit my self and somehow deprive me of my place in it?[44]

Anna is poised on the painful borderline between self-absorption and an openness that is not yet quite closed to love. She searches for the perfect companion, but when the Bridegroom comes along the street—clearly the figure of Christ—she is disconcerted to find in His face the face she hates and fears, the face of Stefan. A process begins in her, as she considers the face of Stefan as it is reflected in the Bridegroom's face and the face of Stefan embodied in her sometime husband. She cannot any longer recover that initial "girlish" infatuation and rapture, since it has "dried up like water which cannot a second time spring from the earth."[45] Nor can she erase the "disproportion" between the faces, which is in fact a disproportion between existence and love.[46] Though the faces are somehow the same, she cannot bring herself to identify them. Still, some healing has begun: with a sense of her own share of

---

44. *The Jeweler's Shop*, act 2, scene 1 (*CP*, p. 294).

45. *The Jeweler's Shop*, act 3, scene 5 (*CP*, p. 319).—The image occurs earlier, as Adam speaks to Anna on behalf of the Bridegroom (Christ): "Beloved, you do not know how deeply you are mine, how much you belong to my love and my suffering—because to love means to give life through death; to love means to let gush a spring of the water of life into the depths of the soul, which burns or smolders and cannot burn out. Ah, the flame and the spring. You don't feel the spring, but are consumed by the flame. Is that not so?" (act 2, scene 3 [*CP*, pp. 305-6]).

46. Adam observes: "Sometimes human existence seems too short for love. At other times, however, it is the other way around: human love is too short in relation to existence—or rather too trivial" (*The Jeweler's Shop*, act 3, scene 5 [*CP*, p. 321]).—Cf. also, act 1, scene 3 (*CP*, p. 288): "A disproportion between the wish for happiness and a man's potential is unavoidable." But, then, too, the Chorus reminds us that, if the disproportion is to be remedied, "Man will not suffice" (act 1, scene 5 [*CP*, p. 292]).

responsibility for the breakup, she arrives at something a little short of forgiveness; and finally, at the sense that she and Stefan have become "less burdensome" in each other's presence. Through her suffering Anna has learned—perhaps better than Stefan—something deeper about the meaning of love. In intimate conversation with Adam—Adam, after all, is somehow in solidarity with her own humanity and with all humanity—she has come to reject her immature notion that love is "a matter of the senses and of a climate which unites and makes two people walk in the sphere of their feeling."[47] And yet, while love is not simply emotion, neither is it thought or imagination cut off from the whole of life. When Anna asks: "With what is thought to remain, then?" Adam replies: "With truth."[48] Thought plays a role in love, but in the end we cannot answer why we love; love is—in dry philosophical terms—the first principle, which gives meaning to everything else. Christopher speaks of his love for Monica:

> Why does one love at all? What do I love you for, Monica? Don't ask me to answer. I couldn't say. Love outdistances its object or approaches it so closely that it is almost lost from view. Man must then think differently, must leave cold deliberations—and in that "hot thinking" one question is important: Is it creative?[49]

If the first theme plays out the relation in love between consciousness and reality, the second probes the depths of love. For love has both surface and depth. Christopher urges Monica to look more deeply into her parents in order to see the love with which they have nourished her: "People have their depths, not only the masks on their faces."[50] Adam, too, finds a paradox in love:

> There is no other matter embedded more strongly in the surface of

---

47. *The Jeweler's Shop*, act 2, scene 2 (*CP*, p. 300).—Earlier Andrew had said: "I simply resisted sensation and the appeal of the senses, for I knew that otherwise I would never really leave my ego and reach the other person—but that meant an effort [of the will] . . . I wanted to regard love as passion, as an emotion to surpass all—I believed in the absolute of emotion" (act 1, scene 1 [*CP*, pp. 280-81]).

48. *The Jeweler's Shop*, act 2, scene 2 (*CP*, p. 300).

49. *The Jeweler's Shop*, act 3, scene 2 (*CP*, p. 313).

50. *The Jeweler's Shop*, act 3, scene 3 (*CP*, pp. 316-17): "All that [caring] cannot pass without leaving a trace."

> human life, and there is no matter more unknown and more mysterious. The divergence between what lies on the surface of the mystery of love constitutes precisely the source of the drama. It is one of the greatest dramas of human existence. The surface of love has its current—swift, flickering, changeable. A kaleidoscope of waves and situations full of attraction. This current is sometimes so stunning that it carries people away—women and men. They get carried away by the thought that they have absorbed the whole secret of love, but in fact they have not yet even touched it. They are happy for a while, thinking they have reached the limits of existence and wrested all its secrets from it, so that nothing remains. That's how it is [in their view]: on the other side of that rapture nothing remains, there is nothing left behind it.

Adam pauses, and with new vehemence, protests: "But there can't be nothing; there can't! Listen to me, there can't. Man is a continuum, a totality and a continuity—so it cannot be that nothing remains."[51]

The conversation turns then upon the relation between the temporal surface of love and its eternal depth. Love is less a matter of time than of eternity.[52] It is not an adventure of the passing moment, since it is shot through with that vertical axis that "cuts across every marriage."[53] Adam's reflection upon the source of love highlights the contrast between surface and depth, adventure and drama, the empty and the full, the part and the whole, the momentary now and the eternal forever. The contrast invites the connection of human love with its source. Adam softly says to Anna: "Ah, Anna, how am I to prove to you that on

---

51. *The Jeweler's Shop*, act 3, scene 3 (*CP*, pp. 301-2).

52. In *The Jeweler's Shop*, act 1, scene 1 (*CP*, p. 279), Teresa notices a certain quality of eternity about love: she recalls the moment when Andrew proposed to her, and observes: "At such moments one does not check the hour, such moments grow in one above time."

53. *The Jeweler's Shop*, act 3, scene 3 (*CP*, p. 316).—Adam to Anna: "Love is not an adventure. It has the flavor of the whole man. It has his weight and the weight of his whole fate. It cannot be a single moment. Man's eternity passes through it. That is why it is to be found in the dimensions of God, because only He is eternity. Man looking out into time, to forget, to forget. To be for a moment only—only now—and cut himself off from eternity. To take in everything at one moment and lose everything immediately after. Ah, the curse of that next moment and all the moments that follow, moments through which he will look for the way back to the moment that has passed, to have it once more, and through it—everything" (act 2, scene 3 [*CP*, p. 303]).—Cf. the despair over the search for the "beautiful moment" in Sartre's *Nausea*.

the other side of all those loves that fill our lives there is Love!"[54] And in his last speech, meditating upon the rift between Anna and Stefan, Adam observes: "The thing is that love carries people away like an absolute, although it [human love] lacks absolute dimensions. But acting under an illusion, they do not try to connect that love with the Love that has such a dimension."[55]

It is not only a matter of the connection between human love and Absolute Love. Within the sphere of human love itself, the love of the parents forms a base in the children and has a hand in shaping their love for one another. Meditating upon the relation between parents and children, Teresa notices "how heavily we all weigh upon their fate. Take Monica's heritage: the rift of that love is so deeply embedded in her that her own love stems from a rift too."[56] It is inevitable, then, that in order to forge their own new love, children must cross the "threshold" of their parents' love "to reach their new homes." It may seem to parents that their children grow inaccessible, like "impermeable soil"; but in truth, she confides, "they have already absorbed us. And though outwardly they shut themselves off, inwardly we remain in them"—for good and/or ill.

Children are marked by the quality of their parents' love for one another. On the one hand, Christopher has been given an "idea of Father"[57] through his mother's continuing love for her dead husband, but he himself has no actual memory of his father. He therefore lacks ready models of manhood, and he does not know "what a man ought to be." Nevertheless, he is called to fatherhood by his love for Monica. Monica, on the other hand, is at first afraid *of* Christopher and afraid *for* herself; but as she falls more deeply in love with him, she reverses the order, and now becomes afraid *of* her inability to love adequately,

---

54. *The Jeweler's Shop*, act 2, scene 3 (*CP*, p. 305).

55. *The Jeweler's Shop*, act 3, scene 5 (*CP*, p. 320). He continues: "They do not even feel the need, blinded as they are not so much by the force of their emotion as by lack of humility. They lack humility toward what love must be in its true essence. The more aware they are of it, the smaller the danger. Otherwise the danger is great: love will not stand the pressure of reality."

56. *The Jeweler's Shop*, act 3, scene 3 (*CP*, p. 314).

57. *The Jeweler's Shop*, act 3, scene 2 (*CP*, p. 311). The reference is to God the Father.—See also *Radiation*, part 1, scene 2 (*CP*, p. 336), where a still defiant Adam worries, "Would people merely associate me always with the idea of the Father?"

and becomes afraid *for* Christopher. She warns him: "You are taking a difficult girl, sensitive to a fault, who easily withdraws into herself and only with effort breaks the circle constantly created by her ego."[58] Christopher can only reply that "love is a constant challenge, thrown to us by God," and in going forward together they must take upon themselves the risk of separation through death (as with Andrew, Christopher's father) or even through estrangement (as with Monica's parents). In his last speech Adam agrees that

> every person has at his disposal an existence and a love. The problem is how to build a sensible structure from it. But this structure must never be inward looking. It must be open in such a way that, on the one hand, it embraces other people, while, on the other, it always reflects the absolute Existence and Love; it must always, *in some way*, reflect them. That is the ultimate sense of your lives.[59]

With that he names each of the six characters personally by name: Teresa! Andrew! Anna! Stefan! and yours: Monica! Christopher!

Meanwhile, Anna and Stefan seem to have made some progress. Through the pain of their separation, each has come to a deeper realization of the demands of love. Anna regrets that she and Stefan have destroyed so much of the basis of trust within Monica. On the other hand, Adam tells us that Anna's encounter with the Bridegroom has awakened in her a new sense of love, a sort of "complementary love," unlike ordinary love. The last speech is left to Stefan, who confesses that he does not understand what it means "to reflect . . . absolute existence and love," but he does realize that he and Anna have in fact reflected love very badly and that their daughter Monica has paid a terrible price for their lack of love. With sudden insight, he turns to Anna and says

---

58. *The Jeweler's Shop*, act 3, scene 2 (*CP*, pp. 311-13).—Teresa had already remarked (act 3, scene I [*CP*, p. 309]): "She was a shy and delicate child—made on me the impression of a being enclosed in herself—whose true value gravitates inward so much that it simply ceases to reach other people."—But Monica's love for Christopher begins to take her out of herself somewhat. Unlike Teresa and Andrew, however, the children take no notice of the Old Jeweler. Monica explains: "We were taken up with each other. . . . All the beauty remained in our own feeling . . . I was absorbed by my love—and by nothing else it seems" (act 3, scene 3 [*CP*, p. 315]).

59. *The Jeweler's Shop*, act 3, scene 5 (*CP*, p 321).

plaintively: "What a pity that for so many years we have not felt ourselves to be a couple of children. Anna, Anna, how much we have lost because of that!"[60]

ର

The last drama is entitled: *Radiation of Fatherhood. A Mystery.*[61] It undoubtedly represents the maturation of Wojtyła's efforts at inner drama. The mystery of humanity evokes the emblem of his own theater of the word and augurs his later anthropology. In a scene between father and child (Adam and Monica) that mystery is embodied in a double image of dense vibrancy. The child is at the edge of a forest in which paths wander, crisscrossing one another, leading to hidden places and mysterious encounters. The father presents himself to his child as carrying about within himself an all-but-impenetrable thicket. Monica asks him: "When will be spoken what is contained in you and me, what lies in the depth of consciousness and must wait for words? Being together, shall we find one day the moments for such words that bring to the surface what really is deep down?"[62] The double image of forest and thicket gives way in the next scene to that of a stream whose current can carry father and child to the inexhaustible Source from which the Fatherhood of love radiates.[63] Józef Tischner remarks that *Radiation of Fatherhood* "attempts to lead us to the origins of all human drama . . . the great metaphysics of a sad physics of our world," "the beautiful but also cruel physics of this world."[64]

---

60. *The Jeweler's Shop*, act 3, scene 5 (*CP*, pp. 319-22).—The theme "You must become as little children . . ." has already emerged in *Our God's Brother* (act 2, scene 2 [*CP*, p. 205]).

61. In 1964 *Znak* published a short piece of poetic prose by A. J. entitled: *Reflections on Fatherhood*. The full drama (written somewhat earlier) under its present title was published in the same journal in Nov. 1979; the drama was performed in Warsaw in June 1983 (See Taborski, *CP*, pp. 323, 327).—Many passages are common, even verbatim, to the prose *Reflections* and the dramatic *Radiation*, and in what follows I will treat them as substantially the same in theme and intent, while noting the source in these notes.

62. *Radiation of Fatherhood*, part 2. "The Experience of a Child," scene 2. "The Child's Sanctuary" (*CP*, p. 346).

63. *Radiation of Fatherhood*, part 2, scene 4 (*CP*, pp. 352ff).

64. From his program notes to the Warsaw production, "Radiation of Creative Interaction," quoted by Taborski, *CP*, pp. 326, 331.

It is not misleading, it seems to me, to characterize the three parts of the drama as follows: In the first we see humanity embodied in Adam as he struggles with his fallen condition. In the second we glimpse the revelation of the trinitarian love within God as it begins to shed its light within the conversation of father and daughter (Adam and Monica), and as it introduces a new energy into their relationship. In the third part we participate with the Mother in humanity's struggle with the hope that has been generated by the promise of fulfillment.

We begin with Adam—the common denominator of humanity—who finds himself exiled from himself, from his deeper personality, and "yet condemned to probe it."[65] The stage is crowded with people, each absorbed in themselves, passing each other by without notice. Adam senses in each person, as well as in himself, the substance of an unrealized humanity; and yet he fears the loss of his own selfhood in the world about him. He fears the loss of self in the transience of the historical process and the anonymity of mass and number that so dominate our modern world. Adam realizes that he must probe the self not from without but from within. And later he insists that "it is not enough to look from the outside," to approach oneself and others as so many objects; but that one must enter within.[66] It comes to this: Adam complains that God might have left him like the other animals, to multiply and flourish on the earth, instead of inflicting upon him something of God's own spiritual personality.[67] But there it is, and we must now take humanity from the inside, from its experiences and not just from its external behavior. Later still, his daughter Monica recalls her father's belated complaint that "too many of the bonds between us are external; there are too few inner bonds."[68] Authentic fatherhood entails an intimate relationship with one's child.

65. *Radiation of Fatherhood*, part 1, scene 1 (*CP*, p. 335). Also in *Reflections on Fatherhood* (*CP*, p. 365).

66. *Radiation of Fatherhood*, part 2, scene 3 (*CP*, p. 347).

67. *Radiation of Fatherhood*, part I, scene 2 (*CP*, p 337): "Did You have to touch my thought with Your knowledge that means giving birth? Did You have to touch my will with the love that is fulfillment?"

68. *Radiation of Fatherhood*, part 2, scene 5 (*CP*, p. 356).

Adam describes himself as Everyman, as the common denominator for that loneliness which humanity has chosen.[69] Indeed, this loneliness is a specific condition, a condition of the species, the elective fate of humankind. We have here, it seems to me, nothing less than a dramatic representation of the fallen situation of man.[70] A certain lethargy sustains this loneliness; Adam finds it easier to feel lonely than to contemplate his actual situation, for that requires him to confront his mortality.[71] He tries to evade his true origin and the call to fatherhood.[72] Excusing himself before God, he pleads: Did I not call from the start, "Leave me my loneliness?"[73] Poised on the border between fatherhood and loneliness, Adam has sought to be more like God; but by this likeness he means: insofar as God is "independent of everything."[74] The conflict is then, if I have understood it correctly, not between an Adam-with-God and an Adam-wholly-without-God, for no creature can exist in the total absence of God. Ultimately Adam's quarrel with God is over two images of God that may define Adam: the image of self-subsistence and the image of relatedness. Adam insists upon choosing the version of self-subsistence. He chooses his own version of what it is to be in the image of God, rather than accepting the actual image that God has conferred upon Adam. Adam chooses the ideal of self-sufficiency

---

69. *Reflections on Fatherhood* (*CP*, pp. 365-66): "Although I am like the man who can be placed apart and then made a common denominator for all men, I still remain lonely." Such objective universality leaves Adam "still a common denominator for everyone, which can be substituted for anyone or a common word that can be put outside the brackets."—In *Radiation of Fatherhood*, part 1, scene 4 (*CP*, p. 339), Adam, speaking to the Father: "When Your Son came, I remained the common denominator of man's inner loneliness."

70. *Radiation of Fatherhood*, part 1, scene 2 (*CP*, p. 336); *Reflections on Fatherhood* (*CP*, p. 365).

71. *Radiation of Fatherhood*, part 1: "Adam," scene 2: "The Analysis of Loneliness" (*CP*, p. 336): "It is easier for me to feel lonely than to think about death. . . . I find it easier to feel lonely than guilty of sin."

72. *Radiation of Fatherhood*, part 1, scene 2 (*CP*, p. 338). Adam admits to "continually evading Your Fatherhood and gravitating toward my loneliness."

73. *Radiation of Fatherhood*, part 1, scene 2 (*CP*, p. 337).

74. *Radiation of Fatherhood*, part 1, scene 2 (*CP*, p. 336); also *Reflections on Fatherhood* (*CP*, p. 365).—In *Radiation*, part 1, scene 2 (*CP*, p. 336): Adam "stopped once on the frontier between fatherhood and loneliness. . . . What if he became lonely of his own free will?"—In the *Original Unity of Man and Woman* (1979-80) John Paul II discusses the "original solitude" of Adam at length; here in the drama Adam hankers after that solitude but on his own terms.

and autonomy, rather than the community of shared love realized in the trinitarian Godhead.[75] Later, Adam concedes that his eyes were too fixed upon himself.[76] He wants to have everything through himself and not through God, even though he knows that such absolute independence is not possible.[77]

At one point Adam tenders God a bargain: Why not split man up into a worldly, outward Adam and an inward, lonely Adam? Into public object and private subject? Into organism and psyche? That, he tells God, would leave the outward Adam to nourish the offspring God seems to desire, while the inward Adam could nurse his own loneliness. And that, Adam concludes, would cleave man in two without touching his inner loneliness.[78] It seems to me that this separation of public externality and private inwardness is pretty much the conventional wisdom put forth by many in our modern world.

Adam finds a strange ambiguity in the word "mine." In its negative sense it means "not yours"; and in the final analysis that means "not God's." The very word itself is relational, even correlative. When it is applied, not simply in an external fashion to the possession of property, but inwardly to the relation between persons, the very word cancels loneliness, because it cannot exclude from its meaning a reference to what is not mine, to what is "yours." And so, against his will, Adam is forced to realize that the very word leads him back towards God. At this point he defiantly decides to abandon the term itself; only to find that the private self is thereby imperiled.[79] For Adam's loneliness is disclosed

---

75. Józef Tischner remarks: "The God of Christianity is not an Absolute Solitude but an Absolute Interaction" of divine Persons (cited in *CP*, p. 327).

76. *Radiation of Fatherhood*, part 1, scene 4: "Between Meeting and Fulfillment" (*CP*, p. 339).

77. *Radiation of Fatherhood*, part 1, scene 2 (*CP*, p. 337). Indeed, Adam pronounces his wish "nonsense," but observes wryly that that has not stopped people from pursuing it.

78. *Radiation of Fatherhood*, part 1, scene 2 (*CP*, p. 337) and scene 4 (*CP*, p. 340).—Cf. (above) Max's "exchangeable" outer man and his inner "non-exchangeable" man in *Our God's Brother*, act 1 (*CP*, pp. 164ff.).

79. *Radiation of Fatherhood*, part 1, scene 2 (*CP*, p. 337): "I am afraid of the word 'mine,' though at the same time I cherish its meaning. . . . An analysis of the word 'mine' always leads me to You. And I would rather give up using it than find its ultimate sense in You" (*Reflections on Fatherhood* [*CP*, p. 366]).—Cf. Psalm 49. It is interesting that the dialectic anticipates, even while it proposes an answer to, the current critique by Derrida and other Deconstructionists, who attack the very notions of the self, authorship, and authority.

as a nullity that loses the very sense of self, either by being driven back into an absolute isolation beyond what is mine or yours, or by being poured out into a common denominator that is neither exclusively mine or yours.

If Adam is lonely by choice, still—as the common denominator of humankind—his loneliness is contagious. Indeed, the emptiness of that common denominator is the basis for the contagion of loneliness. Yet such loneliness is not what God intended when he created human nature. Rather, Adam grafts his loneliness upon others.[80] Later, the figure of the Mother will observe that Adam's children "walk naked from within." Outwardly they are clothed with the products of their own work and with those of other creatures, but "on the inside they are naked."[81]

Because of Adam's self-willed closure—his resistance to God's communication to him and within him—Adam finds the invitation to participate in God's own fatherhood to be not a gift but a burden, an intrusion upon his loneliness.[82] Adam finds it unreasonable of God to want to let his divine Fatherhood enter into Adam's selfhood, for then Adam would reflect the radiation of divine Fatherhood as a prism refracts light. In a word: Adam rejects the burden of carrying the image of God within him and of communicating it to others.[83] He complains that it is too great a risk to be a true father to a child. It is the risk inherent in the call to love, that "constant challenge" of which Christopher has spoken in *The Jeweler's Shop*.[84]

---

80. *Radiation of Fatherhood,* part 1, scene 2 (*CP*, p. 336-37); Adam speaks: "When I give birth, I do it to become lonely among those born, because I pass on to them the germ of loneliness. In the midst of a multitude, are they not more and more lonely?" The use of the word "graft" indicates that the loneliness is an imposition upon human nature and not of its essence: human nature is wounded but not destroyed (also *Reflections on Fatherhood* [*CP*, p. 365]).—Yet such a contagion forms "the strangest community—the community of loneliness" (*Radiation of Fatherhood*, part 3 [*CP*, p. 360]).

81. *Radiation of Fatherhood,* part 3, scene 1 (*CP*, p. 361).

82. *Radiation of Fatherhood,* part 1, scene 2 (*CP*, p. 336): "I could not bear fatherhood; I could not be equal to it. I felt totally helpless—and what had been a gift became a burden to me."

83. *Radiation of Fatherhood,* part 1, scene 2 (*CP*, p. 337). In this context the image relation is one of "mine" and "Yours."

84. *The Jeweler's Shop,* act 3, scene 2 (*CP*, p. 312), "thrown to us by God, thrown, I think, so that we should challenge fate." Fate here is the destiny inherent in our fallen nature, the rule of sin.

Still, Adam struggles with the challenge. He comes to recognize that loneliness is not ultimate in him: "not at the bottom of my being at all." This is because there is a deeper fissure in his being than any subsequent closure, an open sesame into which God makes his way. This fissure is not the rift explored in *The Jeweler's Shop*; for that rift is not original but comes later and not without human choice. Surely, the fissure is the "place" for the influx of the creative existence that sustains Adam at the cutting edge of his being.[85] It is an absolute opening, an opening for the Father's love, that Absolute Love already present in the earlier dramas. Thus, for example, it is the face of her separated husband as it is reflected in the face of the Bridegroom that works upon Anna and gradually makes Stefan's presence "less burdensome" to her.

Adam understands that the opposition founded in conflict is meant to give way to a harmony that endorses his own integrity. But the challenge of love continues, and the risk continues with it. Perhaps we should interpret Adam's struggle as a struggle with that original solitude mentioned in Genesis, prior to the creation of woman. Or rather, the struggle is with what Adam might have suffered had God left him in that solitude. At any rate, Adam seems here to recount his own fall. The very success of creation tempts Adam toward a drift: "Gradually I cease to feel that You express Yourself in me, and I begin to think that I express myself in myself."[86] But then a sense of nonfulfillment arises within Adam, caused—not simply by desire—but by a certain withdrawal from that original Love. A void wells up within him on the borderline of that original-solitude-now-become-loneliness.[87] The void mingles Adam's as-yet-untransformed loneliness with the suffering inseparable from the call to love, a call that is daunting to Adam in his

---

85. *Radiation of Fatherhood*, part 1, scene 3 (*CP*, p. 338); Adam speaks: ". . . You are never against me. You enter into what I call loneliness, and You overcome my resistance. Can one say that You force Your way in or only that You enter through a door that is open anyway? You did not make me closed; You did not quite close me. Loneliness is not at the bottom of my being at all; it grows at a certain point. The fissure through which You enter is far deeper. You enter—and slowly begin to shape me. You shape and develop me in spite of what I imagine about my ego and other people, yet You do it in harmony with what I am."

86. *Radiation of Fatherhood*, part 1, scene 3 (*CP*, p. 338).

87. *Radiation of Fatherhood*, part 1, scene 2. (*CP*, p. 338); Adam is poised "between the upper borderline of man filled with humanity and the lower one of humanity destroyed in man."

loneliness. For the suffering arises only through the muted presence of a Love whose absence is nevertheless felt and somehow understood.[88]

It is here that a pivotal scene takes up the theme of "The Threshold Crossed by Woman." The Woman is undoubtedly Eve, but also Everywoman and each woman; is she also Mary? and the Church? At any rate, she enters Adam's loneliness perhaps at several levels, so that Adam is able to move from the pole of loneliness toward the pole of love.[89] The Woman conceives a child and gives to Adam a new sense of "mine," that very sense which he had resisted. He had resisted because, while his own fatherhood would break down his loneliness, it would also lead him to the Father whose very being is Fatherhood. It is through the child, then, that Adam becomes a father. He says, half complaining: "You want me to love. You aim at me through a child, through a tiny daughter or son—and my resistance weakens."[90]

But Adam arrives at a deeper truth, a truth that arises out of his not-entirely-willing recognition of the image of God that is present in him through the fissure. He realizes that the radiation of the Father's love consists in giving birth, even as from all eternity the Father is Father through begetting His Son: "We return to the father through the child."[91] What is more, Adam comes to realize that—according to the logic of existence embedded in everything—he can accept the radiation of Love from the Father in and through the Son, only by therewith

---

88. *Radiation of Fatherhood,* part 2, scene 4 (*CP,* p. 353). Adam to Monica: "Every feeling, my child, must be permeated by light. . . . One must transfix feelings with thought."

89. *Radiation of Fatherhood,* part 3, scene 1 (*CP,* p. 360). It seems to me that, at the first entrance (*Radiation,* part 1, scene 3, *CP,* p. 339), the Woman is Eve and Everywoman, but that here she is the Woman of Faith, hence Mary and the Church, and whoever—woman and men—live out of that faith.

90. *Radiation of Fatherhood,* part 1, scene 3 (*CP,* p. 338). The same holds for the Mother (*CP,* p. 339). And at part 3, scene 1 (*CP,* p. 362), speaking to the newborn child, the Woman says: "This is also the moment of my birth, the moment in which I become a Mother." Although Adam's resistance is weakened, he still warns Monica: "Is it not true that in the word 'father' there is also fear? I will never be only stillness but also storm. Nor will I be sweetness only; I will add bitterness. And though I try to be transparent, I will also be a puzzle" (part 2, scene 5 [*CP,* p. 356]). Earlier the Chorus asks: "Where has the exiled father gone to? Where has the punishing father come from?" (part 1, scene 4 [*CP,* p. 340]). It is possible that these words, once transformed by that Absolute Love Who is Mercy, might also adumbrate the divine Father.

91. *Radiation of Fatherhood,* part 1, scene 5 (*CP,* p. 341).

becoming himself a son, and once again a child: "To absorb the radiation of fatherhood means not only to become a father but, much more, to become a child."[92] Adam says: "After a long time I came to understand that you do not want me to become a father unless I become a child."[93] The image within Adam is the image of "my" Father and "yours," Who has begotten the Word, and of his Spirit who proceeds from their Love. Father, child and love: that is what is essential, what remains.[94]

Throughout the drama the Mother—especially in the third and last part—remains a mysterious figure; perhaps the author intended it so. If on her first entrance she may be mostly Eve, or Everywoman and each woman, in the last part she seems also to stand for the Church, and within the Church for Mary. She speaks of herself as the least obtrusive of the servants of history, bringing to mind the *Magnificat*.

Already in part two, in the child's sanctuary, we find that the stream, which is at once the edge of earth and of human thought, is not an ordinary stream. Just after being rescued from a viper on the trail, Monica puts her feet in the cool, refreshing water of the forest stream: it is "the water that has given birth to man anew"—surely a reference to baptism.[95]

Moreover, the Mother is not herself the light, since that Light radiates from the Father; but she is the shade that protects, and she herself glows with an inner radiance which she communicates to the children of Adam.[96] Each time, she counsels: "Adam, accept the radiation of

---

92. *Reflections on Fatherhood* (*CP*, p. 368). Cf. Stefan to Anna, *The Jeweler's Shop*, act 3, scene 5 (*CP*, pp. 319-22). The insistence upon becoming once again a child undoubtedly follows from Jesus' injunction: "Unless you become as little children. . . ." In sharp contrast to Wojtyła's emphasis, Descartes all but complains that we would have been better off if from the start we had been born with fully adult human reasons (*Discourse* I-II), and Kant in his essay *What is Enlightenment?* holds forth the escape from dependency (tutelage) as the beginning of mature humanity.

93. *Radiation of Fatherhood*, part 1, scene 4 (*CP*, p. 339). What is more, in the constant giving of birth, "the father revives [as father] in the soil of the child's soul" (*CP*, p. 340).

94. *Radiation of Fatherhood*, part 3, scene 2 (*CP*, p. 364). Also *Reflections on Fatherhood* (*CP*, p. 368): "And everything else will then turn out to be unimportant and inessential, except for this: father, child, and love."—It seems that the secret formula of which Adam speaks at *Radiation* part 2, scene 5 (*CP*, p. 358) is the Trinity; cf. n. 75.

95. *Radiation of Fatherhood*, part 2, scene 3 (*CP*, p. 350).

fatherhood; Adam, become a child." But each time Adam is silent; he does not hear or want to hear. She expresses her fatigue more than once toward the close of the drama, and at one point she whispers: "Oh, Adam, how tired I am of you. Truly, fatigue is the measure of our love." But she answers the call of the Bridegroom, and calls in turn to Adam's children to "take into yourself the light that will guide you through Adam's loneliness and lead you to the Father."[97]

Now, Adam knows that the love she communicates to all humankind liberates men and women from loneliness. Indeed, it liberates from an unattached freedom, and gives rise to a new, more certain freedom.[98] For the fullness of God is the denial of the emptiness of loneliness.[99] But Adam also realizes that the same light leads straight through the Invisible Child who rests in the Mother's arms, and that it must pass through the suffering and death of that Child, as well as through the death of all human fatherhood and human childhood. And with that Adam is brought back to the thought he has tried to evade throughout the drama: the realization of his mortality.

A troubled Adam remains poised in a quandary between two choices: the loneliness of his own self-isolation, or the adopted fatherhood-childhood that must pass through suffering and death. Adam has known all these things: he has known that the Father is the Source who shows the way, and that the Father could retreat without loss within the

---

96. *Radiation of Fatherhood,* part 3, scene 1, "Concern for Inner Radiance" (*CP,* pp. 360-61). The Mother: "I gather the people whom Adam has dispersed. There is in me a love stronger than loneliness. That love is not of me. . . . I love Adam and constantly restore to him the fatherhood he renounces. I discreetly turn his loneliness into my motherhood. . . . And I am not the light of those I enlighten but rather a shade in which they rest. . . . I do not know how it happens that I fill these people with radiance from within. Or rather I do know, but my knowledge is faith."

97. *Radiation of Fatherhood,* part 3, scene 1 (*CP,* p. 362). It is here that she adds, "This is also the moment of my birth, the moment in which I become a Mother."

98. *Radiation of Fatherhood,* part 2, scenes 4-5 (*CP,* pp. 355-56): "Love denies freedom of will to him who loves—love liberates him from the freedom that would be terrible to have for its own sake. . . . What remains is to await a new maturity, a new unity of will, a common rhythm . . . when we love, a common current runs through our wills. From it a certainty grows, and freedom is born again from certainty. And this is what love means. And then without fear I think 'mine'."

99. *Reflections on Fatherhood* (*CP,* p. 368).

Godhead to the absolute Love between Father and Child, leaving the whole world to its self-destruction. The chorus echoes Adam's desperate sigh: "Could we not have learned this long ago? Has this not always been embedded in everything that is?"[100] But the drama closes with the Mother's clarion voice: "You are wrong, Adam! You are all wrong! In me will survive the heritage of all men, implanted in the Bridegroom's death."

In *Reflections on Fatherhood,* Adam says: "All this I know. But is it enough? Knowing, I can continue to substitute for everything the same old common denominator of my loneliness—my inner loneliness, chosen so that I can remain myself alone and nobody else."[101] And again, in his conversation with Monica, Adam asks, "When we descend from word to will, what will the word mean?"[102]

We are left at the close of the drama, then, with an indecisive Adam, a sort of universal Hamlet; he needs something more than the knowledge he has: he needs to *act.*[103]

---

100. *Radiation of Fatherhood,* part 3, scene 2, "Radiation and Dying" (*CP*, p. 368). *Reflections on Fatherhood* (*CP*, p. 368) closes on this note.

101. *Reflections on Fatherhood* (*CP*, p. 368). Is this not the same "knowledge without love" against which (in *Our God's Brother*) the future Brother Albert protests to the Other, i.e., to the voice of the Enlightenment? Or again, in *Jeremiah,* when Father Peter cries out that "words are not enough!"

102. *Radiation of Fatherhood,* part 2, scene 5 (*CP*, p. 357). It is not too much to see here a dramatic form of Wojtyła's philosophical concern with ethical action and its foundations.

103. In *Rhapsodies of the Millennium* (*CP*, pp. 385-86) Wojtyła illustrates the drama of moral values by reference to the legend of Mieczyslaw in which a newly Christian people's collective action topples the statue of the "god" Światowid. At once horrified yet determined, proud yet humble, they tremble before the unseen consequences of the act. This, he observes, is "a drama of the highest order, a drama in the sphere of values." And in *Forefathers' Eve* (*CP*, p. 389) he speaks of a "theater of specific action," of "multidimensional action," and of the moral task of such drama.

BOLESŁAW TABORSKI

Bolesław Taborski, poet, translator, award-winning writer, and expert on theatre, was born in Toruń, Poland, in 1927. When World War II broke out, he was closely involved with the underground theatre in Kraków and later moved to Warsaw, where he attended clandestine high school classes, joined the armed resistance against occupying Nazi German forces, and took part in the Warsaw Rising of 1944. After the fall of the uprising, he was held captive in a POW camp in Germany, which was liberated by British forces at the end of the War. He made his way to London, England, where, after graduating from the University of Bristol in English and Drama, he worked as a radio journalist and broadcaster for the BBC World Service. He was also a visiting professor at the City University of New York. He started writing poetry in his early teens, and had twenty-four volumes of poetry published. He also translated literary works from Polish into English and vice versa, wrote an award-winning book on the Warsaw Rising, a number of books on the theatre, and two Polish-language books on Karol Wojtyła as poet and playwright: *Karola Wojtyły dramaturgia wnętrza (Karol Wojtyła's dramaturgy of the interior)* (1989) and *Wprost w moje serce uderza droga wszystkich (Straight into my heart strikes the path of all)* (2005). He had a personal friendship with Pope John Paul II, which grew out of their shared interest in literature and the fact that Taborski was chosen as translator of Karol Wojtyła's plays into English by a special Papal Commission. Taborski was a member of the Polish Writers' Association and PEN. He died in London, in 2010, leaving behind his wife Halina and daughter Anna.

CPMAP Certification

CPMAP stands for the *CatholicPsych Model of Applied Personalism.*

We developed the CPMAP Certification over the last ten years in training Catholic therapists by integrating the work of St. John Paul II with the science of psychology. His contributions to psychology and philosophy of the person should be front and center in any Catholic training model.

For the first time ever, the same integrated Psychological training used to prepare our CatholicPsych licensed therapists is available to therapy and non-therapy helpers alike!

Our training is now for those in ministry, mental-health professions, leadership positions, missionary work, and even family life who regularly confront the suffering of others.

Our certification trains you to accompany people burdened in areas of mental and spiritual health through the *integration* of Catholic philosophy, traditional spirituality, and relevant psychology woven together to understand...

How We're Made • How We're Wounded • How We're Healed

Pope Francis called the Church a "field hospital" in the world today. He was calling all of us to accompany others with this mindset. How can we run field hospitals without training the medics?

Learn more about our CPMAP Certification at

www.iddmentor.com/openhouse?sts